COLORADO UFOS

COLORADO UFOS

RICHARD ESTEP

Schiffer
Publishing Ltd

4880 Lower Valley Road • Atglen, PA 19310

For my friend Dave Schrader
and his Army of Darkness

artwork by Chuck Chroma

Type set in Univers &

ISBN: 978-0-7643-5640-7

Printed in China

Published by Schiffer Publishing, Ltd.
4880 Lower Valley Road
Atglen, PA 19310
Phone: (610) 593-1777; Fax: (610) 593-2002
E-mail: Info@schifferbooks.com
Web: www.schifferbooks.com

For our complete selection of fine books on this and related subjects, please visit our website at www.schifferbooks.com. You may also write for a free catalog.

Schiffer Publishing's titles are available at special discounts for bulk purchases for sales promotions or premiums. Special editions, including personalized covers, corporate imprints, and excerpts, can be created in large quantities for special needs. For more information, contact the publisher.

We are always looking for people to write books on new and related subjects. If you have an idea for a book, please contact us at proposals@schifferbooks.com.

CONTENTS

FOREWORD

At 8:30 p.m. on the evening of February 25, 2012, the air was cool, as the sun had set a only few hours before. The sky was free of clouds, and the tiny sliver of moon was rising. The lack of any real wind prevented the particulate matter over Colorado's Front Range urban corridor from dispersing. Consequently, the multitude of aircraft in the skies took on the appearance of moving sodium vapor lights high in the sky. It was on this night that I was driving eastbound on my way to Fort Lupton.

Traffic was unusually sparse for the time, which provided multiple opportunities to gaze up at the sky above the road and marvel at the coordinated dance of these deep, dirty-yellow lights transiting the skies. It was at one of these moments that something caught my attention in my forward field of view. Alone on the road, I took my foot off the accelerator, slowing slightly.

Fifty degrees above the horizon, three planes were converging. From my vantage point it gave the illusion that they might collide. Suddenly, all three flew upward and formed the Atari logo, halting at the top. I was mystified. I stepped on the brake and stopped my Jeep, amazed at what I was seeing. After a very brief moment the lights descended, retracing their flight pattern, flew off in various directions, and quickly blended in with the rest of the air traffic in the skies.

For almost a minute I sat there, parked in the middle of the lonely highway, wondering what I'd witnessed. Oncoming headlights brought me back to my current situation, and I continued on my journey, wondering what it was that I saw. When I arrived at my destination, I queried the people assembled—the author Richard Estep and his paranormal investigation team—to see if they had witnessed this event. No one had, but one reported that unusual airborne sightings were the norm in Fort Lupton due to the relative proximity to various airports.

My own interest in the UFO phenomenon started in the early 1970s, but it wasn't until 2005 that I decided to go beyond simply consuming books and videos. I joined MUFON, the Mutual UFO Network, which is billed as "the world's oldest and largest UFO phenomenon investigative body."

Through MUFON's website, www.mufon.com, they provide UFO news and research as well as allow people to submit UFO sighting reports which are then investigated by MUFON field investigators. It takes commitment to become a field investigator for MUFON. One has to:

- Obtain, study, and pass a very long and detailed test based upon the hefty field investigator manual
- Join the organization
- Complete field investigator-specific legal paperwork
- Complete the field investigator on-boarding plan, which includes additional training
- Complete an interview with the local director, ostensibly designed to weed out any bad apples that have gotten this far in the process, as well as to arrange a personal, ongoing training plan
- Assemble, at your own expense, a field investigator go-kit for on-site work
- Participate in a supervised field training program until the local director deems you ready
- Maintain their skills by independently leading investigations as well as various continuing educational requirements

Those in law enforcement will notice this closely mirrors the process used to train new police officers. This is by design with the intent to produce a highly skilled and self-sufficient individual. To top it off, MUFON investigators are unpaid and unreimbursed volunteers. Due to the above requirements, it is easy to understand why there are a limited amount of field investigators. Only those detail-oriented individuals with steadfast commitment weather the test of time. It was this role that I was to eventually take on. In doing so, I was exposed to a facet of Colorado that the general public has little mainstream awareness of.

Centralized UFO investigation in Colorado is orchestrated by the local MUFON chapter (www.comufon.org). The chapter holds monthly public events, as well as membership meetings and training. Colorado's team of field investigators average just under 200 cases per year, although since 2015, there has been a roughly fifteen percent increase in yearly case reports.

An average of ten cases per year are high-priority "Category 3" cases, which include reports of contactees and abductees. These cases require extensive field work, including documentation, evidence collection, and extensive witness interviews. These cases, with documented evidence, are often picked up by MUFON's science team, comprised of eminent professional specialists in a wide variety of fields, for further investigation. Unfortunately, hoaxes—and hoaxers—are still quite common and are the bane of the field investigation team. Valuable time is spent investigating reports only to uncover insufficient or contradictory evidence to support the claims.

Thankfully, in Colorado the number of hoaxes is comparatively low, averaging fifteen per year. More than fifty-five percent of cases are ultimately determined to be IFOs (identified flying objects). The majority of these are man-made objects such as various types of aircraft. Aviation has a significant economic impact in Colorado: It accounts for 265,700 jobs, $12.6 billion in payrolls, and a total economic output of $36.7 billion, according to the latest study by the Colorado Division of Aeronautics.

In addition to large commercial hubs, such as Denver International Airport, there are sixty airports and 447 heliports in Colorado communities not served by commercial airlines. Colorado also has six known military bases, all with aviation elements. Needless to say, there is significant and constant airborne activity in Colorado.

UFO sightings in Colorado happen across the state. According to a 2015 article using data from www.theblackvault.com, Saguache County is the county with the most reports, averaging 96.77 sightings per 100,000 people. Park, Alamosa, Huerfano, and Chaffee counties are not far behind. Beyond UFO sightings, Colorado has its own share of chemtrail reports, cattle mutilation, healthy speculation of various hidden extraterrestrial bases, engaging evidence of a deep underground bunker at Denver International Airport, and the aptly named UFO Watchtower located in Saguache County. All of these combine to make Colorado a very interesting place for UFO enthusiasts.

Some of MUFON's cases end up as news reports on MUFON's website or on shows, such as *Hangar 1*, but most cases, which can be searched via the MUFON website, are not covered by the mainstream media. In addition, MUFON only receives what is believed to be a small fraction of all UFO experiences: Most go unreported and uninvestigated. The true scope of what people are witnessing is unknown.

Books, such as the one you are now holding, offer a window into a hidden world. Your author, Richard Estep, is no stranger to hidden worlds. In addition to being a well-published author, he has been active as a paranormal investigator for many years. I can attest to his methodical approach, having joined him on many investigations. Richard's paranormal experience brings a different perspective to the UFO scene, allowing him to both report on evidence and witness testimony as well as entertain the reader with experience-based speculation.

In this book, Richard has pulled together the experiences of individual UFO witnesses, contactees, and abductees in the state of Colorado as seen through his unique lens. In addition to entertaining you, this book will open your mind to both rational and plausible explanations as well as exploring the mysterious and unknown activity in the skies above Colorado. It's my wish that Richard's success with this book will lead him to write many more and entertain us, his readers, with his distinctive style and perspective.

Joey Stanford
MUFON Field Investigator

February 20, 2017
Longmont, Colorado

PREFACE

All right. You got me. I'll admit it. I'm not the most obvious person to write a book about UFOs.

I've spent the past twenty years as a paranormal investigator, looking into claims of haunted places, objects, and people on both sides of the Atlantic. That segued rather naturally into my writing books about the paranormal, with an emphasis on ghosts and hauntings. When the good people at Schiffer Publishing read through my proposal for another ghost book, they showed a polite interest—but said that what they *really* wanted was a book on the subject of UFOs in my adopted state of Colorado.

"Don't rehash the same old reports and troll from existing websites," I was cautioned when we were laying down the parameters of the book. They wanted to see some contemporary research. How were things in the UFO scene trending in the Mile High City and its surrounding environs?

To tell you the truth, that came as a huge relief to me. I wasn't really interested in writing out a list of UFO sightings in chronological order and trying desperately to add some meat to those same tired old bones. I'm also pretty sure that you, dear reader, wouldn't be all that interested in handing over your hard-earned cash for such a book. Not when the same information could be easily gleaned by a Google search.

Fortunately, I wasn't a total novice. The subject of UFOs had always fascinated me, and I'd read enough to be able to hold my own in a conversation about Rendlesham Forest, Roswell, Socorro, Travis Walton, Barney and Betty Hill, and many of the other pillars that have supported ufology for decades. I had also been struck by the commonalities that seemed to exist between my own field of paranormal research and those of ufology: orbs/lights, apparitions, and astral travel, to name but a few. It quickly became clear that the Don Quixote-like task of the paranormal investigator and the UFO investigator had more similarities than they did differences. Perhaps I wasn't so unqualified after all.

It's impossible to talk about the Colorado UFO scene without discussing certain things. One is the Denver International Airport, which always seems to head the list of conspiracy and ufology-type news articles regarding Colorado. Another is what is arguably the first well-documented cattle mutilation, that of "Snippy" back in 1967. The story is still widely told today, accompanied by a fascinating set of animal bones, and holds a genuine fascination for a great many people.

Snippy's story led me to the subject of animal mutilation in general and opened the door for me to interview one of the world's leading researchers on that subject, the affable Christopher O'Brien. When we were finished delving into the murky subject of mutilation, Christopher and I went on to discuss his work investigating UFO sightings in Colorado's mystical San Luis Valley.

Of course, one cannot visit the San Luis Valley without stopping off at the famed UFO Watchtower. What some regarded as a joke when it was first built back in 2000, has now become a genuine UFO hotspot, the site of many well-attested sightings, not to mention visits from some who claim to be of extraterrestrial origins themselves. Its owner, Judy Messoline, took great joy in relating the ups and downs of her sixteen years spent running this exceptional UFO-spotting platform.

When the word got out among my friends, colleagues, and readers on social media that I was writing a book on the UFO phenomenon as it relates to Colorado, some of them started to come out of the woodwork with their own personal experiences. One fascinating case occurred to my friend Lucilla's mother, back in the 1980s. Her story had all the hallmarks of a classic UFO abduction: She was the single occupant of a car driving home on a lonely, isolated stretch of road late at night. There is the bright light in the sky, the car interior illuminating itself, and then the period of missing time on what would turn out to be a truly "interrupted journey." I simply could not fail to include her story once I had heard it in its entirety.

As I conducted more interviews with those who believed that they had seen UFOs, one thing naturally led to another, until I was finally interviewing those who claimed to be experiencing their own "Close

Encounters of the Fourth Kind": actual abduction by the occupants of those alien craft. I have no doubt that the section that covers the Colorado-based contactees and abductees shall be the most controversial; it also comprises the lion's share, simply because the experiences of men such as "Al" (a pseudonym) and Don, and ladies such as Sierra, make for such engrossing—if admittedly fantastical—reading. Some will doubtless find the stories these people have to tell to be simply too hard to swallow, dismissing them out of hand as either fiction or the ramblings of a delusional mind. For my part, all that I can tell you is that I sat down with each of these people, looked them in the eyes as they told me their stories and answered my questions, and saw no deception there. Whether or not you believe their stories is for you to decide. I can only tell you that *they* most certainly believe it.

In writing the book, I have endeavored to show both sides of the coin when it comes to the abduction phenomenon. For some of the abductees/contactees, such as Al, the experience has been nothing short of a curse, bringing along with it a host of physical and emotional difficulties that have plagued him for decades. For others, such as Sierra and Don, quite the reverse is true; their lives have been enriched by their interaction with the extraterrestrials, to the point where they would not trade the experience for the world. And then there is a third group, as evidenced by Stan, for whom the whole thing has been very much a double-edged sword.

The further into the phenomenon I delved, the more people I interviewed, the more questions seemed to arise.

Are there really, as some contactees claim, either hundreds of thousands or even *millions* of alien beings walking among us, hiding in plain sight and interacting with us on a daily basis?

Are the so-called "Greys" extraterrestrial beings intent upon doing humanity ill, or the inhabitants of a parallel Earth who are desperately trying to gather genetic material from us, as part of an interbreeding program that will allow them to repopulate their own devastated planet?

We will try and make sense of these, and many other questions, as we go along.

While it is true that the original remit of the book was to be confined to the great state of Colorado, it soon became apparent that the scope of the book was going to be greater than that. It increased just a little bit in scale. To *galactic* proportions, you might say. Having spoken with Al, Sierra, and Don at great length, it soon became clear to me that I was working on a much bigger canvas than merely one state, in one country, on one continent, on one planet; the backdrop to our story now took in other star systems and other dimensions, not to mention the myriad of alien races that many of the contactees insisted were the inhabitants of such places.

I am under no illusion that this book will change the minds of any skeptics out there, and nor does it try to do so. However, I did want to cover at least one high-profile UFO case in which the skeptical (i.e. non-extraterrestrial) viewpoint may well be the correct one. Just what exactly *were* the mysterious objects that were sighted in the skies above the ski resort of Breckenridge in 2014? The answer may turn out to be a mundane (though no less fascinating) one, but at least one of the eyewitnesses to the event remains convinced to this day that the objects he saw were not of this world.

If you are looking for absolute, definitive answers to this most fascinating of mysteries, then I am afraid that this book is going to disappoint. After interviewing eyewitness from all walks of life, I am still no closer to figuring out exactly what *I* believe lies at the heart of the UFO phenomenon. Some of the material presented within these pages will no doubt seem far-fetched to many readers, and to that I can only reply with, "Guilty as charged!" I have not diluted or altered the testimonies of my interview subjects, no matter how difficult to believe they may appear to be, choosing instead to simply present them to you, the reader, so that you may formulate your own opinion.

The UFO phenomenon continues to thrill, fascinate, intrigue, and beguile us. Interest in what may turn out to be the biggest of all unanswered questions shows no signs of slowing down as the twenty-first century gains traction. If some of the people who you will meet among the pages of this book are correct, then the human race is about to enter a period of explosive transformation the likes of which history has never seen. Extraterrestrial intervention in human affairs may reach an all-time high in the very near future.

It must also be noted that governmental disclosure may finally become a reality, rather than a pipe dream. When I first started this book, the electoral race was in full swing. Hillary Clinton was speaking about "getting to the bottom" of the UFO phenomenon. Her campaign chair, John Podesta, had expressed an interest in the subject more than once in the past, and was openly stating that the United States government could be doing a much better job about feeding information on UFOs to the American people—a statement with which, I suspect, the vast majority of us would agree.

Would President Hillary Clinton really have broken down the wall of silence surrounding the UFO phenomenon? We will never know, it seems, as Donald Trump would subsequently go on to occupy the Oval Office, but Podesta certainly seemed to think that she would. "What I've talked to the secretary about, and what she's said now in public, is that if she's elected president, when she gets into office, she'll ask for as many records as the United States federal government has to be declassified, and I think that's a commitment that she intends to keep and that I intend to hold her to," he said in an interview with CNN. "The American people can handle the truth."

Let's hope that someday, no matter who occupies the highest office of the land, the American people finally get the opportunity to find out.

CHAPTER 1.

ON A LONELY ROAD

The UFO phenomenon, along with so many other space and science fiction-related matters, was at the very forefront of the American public consciousness in 1982. We have Hollywood to largely thank for that: This was the summer of the blockbuster, when movies such as *Star Trek II: The Wrath of Khan,* John Carpenter's *The Thing, Blade Runner,* and *Tron* ruled movie theaters and drive-ins from coast to coast . . . not to mention the great-granddaddy of them all, Steven Spielberg's classic story of a friendly alien left behind on Earth, *E. T. The Extra-Terrestrial.*

Stepping out of the darkness of the movie theater and back into the real world, NASA flew three space shuttle missions that same year: one in March, one in June, and one in November. Younger readers may find this hard to believe, but space shuttle launches and landings were a big deal back in the eighties, often meriting live television coverage with expert commentary.

One strange and fascinating incident of which the American public was most definitely *not* aware took place in the Soviet Union in early October. This was the kind of story that Hollywood screenwriters might have dreamed up themselves, because a giant UFO hovering over a Soviet military base located in the Ukraine came perilously close to triggering World War III.

This was the height of the Cold War, when tensions between East and West were close to breaking point. Both NATO and the USSR had a sufficient number of nuclear-tipped warheads pointing at one another's cities and military bases to destroy the entire world many times over, ending civilization (and most likely, human life) on this planet, for all time.

According to the incredulous Russian servicemen who witnessed the incredible episode, the massive UFO—some five stories high, 900 meters wide, and shaped like the classic disc—floated silently into position above the launch silos for their inter-continental ballistic missiles (ICBMs) and simply hovered there, waiting, for the better part of an hour. More ominous even than that, officers who were present at the time have testified that the occupants of the UFO had managed to somehow circumvent the rigorous security systems and robust overrides that were in place. The nukes suddenly *armed themselves,* spinning up into their launch cycle as though somebody (or some*thing*) was preparing to hurl them against their pre-set targets in the United States and Europe.

Had that happened, millions would have died in the initial strike alone: not to mention the cataclysmic death toll that would have followed as NATO forces responded and launched their own flock of lethal nuclear-tipped birds against the Soviets.

The result: Global Armageddon.

With their hearts pounding away like jackhammers inside their chests, the sweating missile control officers and enlisted men watched the end of the world take shape before their helpless eyes. Then, just a few seconds after the missiles had flipped themselves over into launch mode, the brightly-lit control panels suddenly became dark and lifeless. Power drained from the nukes and dissipated, eliciting sighs of relief from all who were gathered there inside the silos.

Over on the other side of the Atlantic, UFO activity was no less common. Ufologist Budd Hopkins had published his seminal work, *Missing Time: A Documented Study of UFO Abductions,* just the year before, helping to bring the phenomenon of alien abduction into the public eye. Just five years before, the advertising campaign of Steven Spielberg's classic *Close Encounters of the Third Kind* had entreated Americans to "Watch the skies," and they had done so ever since, with some even going so far as to report their UFO sightings and abduction experiences to the Mutual UFO Network (MUFON) for inclusion in their massive international database.

The scene has now been set for our next alien encounter, as related to me by a lady named Lucilla about her mother Kathy. Kathy was a wife, homemaker, and the mother of three young children. In addition to being a hard worker, Kathy also had a heart of gold, and it was the confluence of these two character traits that led to her helping out friends of her children by assisting with their school fundraisers. Kathy had a passion for bingo, and particularly liked to be the caller, taking the numbered balls from the machine at the bingo hall in Denver, and reading them out to the audience of players.

Sometimes Kathy's husband would accompany her for a game or two, but more often than not, he would stay home to watch the children while his wife drove to Denver alone.

On one weekend night in 1982, Lucilla remembers watching TV with her dad and siblings, spending some quality family time and waiting for their mom to get home. It was a bingo night, a chance for her mom to have some fun and let her hair down a little, and nobody could begrudge her that; but as the clock crept closer to midnight, father and children alike grew increasingly apprehensive. The family lived in the town of Fort Lupton, and it wasn't all that long of a drive from Denver. Kathy was usually home by eleven o'clock at the latest. Now she was almost an hour late, and they were beginning to worry.

Midnight came and went. Lucilla's father was starting to worry, though he tried to hide it from the kids. Then 12:15 arrived. He got up and began to pace, attempting to work off some of the stress and tension by walking from one end of the kitchen to the other, and then back again.

Finally, at 12:30, Lucilla heard a key turn in the lock. Her father rushed to the door, flinging it wide. Kathy was standing there silently, her face wearing a strange expression.

"Where have you been?" he asked, wrapping her up in a great big hug. The relief came off him in waves that were almost palpable. "We've been worried sick about you!"

Kathy began to cry quietly, tears streaking her face. Taking her by the hand, Lucilla's father led Kathy past the three children and gently escorted her into the bedroom, closing the door firmly behind them. To this day, Lucilla does not know what her parents said to one another behind that closed door, but after a while both of her parents emerged, and Kathy invited the three children to join her at the kitchen table.

"I'm okay," she said reassuringly, looking into each of their faces in turn, "but I need to tell you guys what happened. Don't be scared." Despite her best attempts at comforting her children, Lucilla could see that her mother was quite visibly upset: She was shaking, and something about her just wasn't right. This, in turn, only served to frighten the already-freaked-out children even more, but between them, both parents were able to quieten them enough for Kathy to get her story out.

Kathy had left the bingo hall at around 10:30, her usual time, which normally meant that she would be home around eleven o'clock. The family lived on a farm some five miles east of Fort Lupton, and the only way to access the Interstate was via a series of back roads that were pretty much deserted at night. Kathy was heading home on County Road 37 that night and had nothing more on her mind than getting home to see her husband and children. She wasn't intoxicated, and didn't have any medical or behavioral conditions that might explain what happened next.

Keeping a watchful eye on the road and sticking religiously to the posted speed limit, Kathy hummed a little tune to keep herself company. All of a sudden, she noticed that her car was beginning to slow down. Puzzled, she pushed her foot down harder on the accelerator, but it made no difference. One minute, the car was cruising smoothly, other than hitting the occasional bump; the next, it had slowed to a complete stop at the side of the road, and all without the brake pedal having been used once.

Then the interior of the car was bathed in a deep red light. Kathy was a courageous and hardy woman who was not easily given to fear—she thought nothing of heading out to shoot snakes on the farm with her trusty .38—and yet she was now deeply afraid, and crouched low down into the front seat, trying to make herself as small and unobtrusive a target as she possibly could. Nobody was visible in the area, but she listened to her newfound sense of fear.

Something just wasn't right. She could feel it in her bones.

After what seemed like ages, the red light was suddenly gone, disappearing as quickly as it had arrived. Kathy looked down at her wrist, turning it so that she could see the face of her watch. It had stopped dead at 11:30, the second hand frozen immobile between the two main hands.

It couldn't be 11:30. It felt somehow later than that, although if pressed, Kathy couldn't have said exactly why. She had no recollection of what had happened during the period in which the red light had suffused the inside of her car, illuminating the steering wheel and dashboard in an eerie glow. It was as if the car and its lone occupant had been caught in some kind of beam or ray; Kathy knew that the idea sounded like something that would come straight out of a science fiction movie or a pulp paperback, but there wasn't any better way to describe it.

Reaching down with a trembling hand to turn the ignition key, Kathy was relieved to find that the car started up on the very first try.

Clustered around the table, Kathy's family listened to her story with open mouths and equally open minds. Try as they might, none of them could come up with a rational explanation for what had taken place that night, stealing at least an hour of their mother's life away from her without her permission. The only answer that seemed to fit all the facts was that, like so many other members of the American public, she had undergone an unexpected encounter with a UFO.

As for whatever had happened to her while she was caught inside the red beam, Kathy had not the faintest idea, and to her dying day she would never recall the events of that particular segment of missing time. It was almost as if a surgeon had somehow taken a scalpel and neatly cut out that particular block of memory, excising with great care the record of whatever had taken place out on that lonely and isolated stretch of road.

If there were any signs of trauma or physical evidence on Kathy's body after that late-night interrupted journey, she made no mention of it to any of her children. Lucilla very clearly remembers her mother telling people about the mysterious episodes for many years afterward. Her account never wavered or varied; many tales grow in the telling, but Kathy's story remained completely consistent, sticking to the plain, unembellished facts each time she told it.

There was no saucer-shaped craft, nor were there any Greys or other alien figures, but Kathy's story bears all the characteristics of an alien encounter . . . particularly when one considers a final piece of information surrounding the case.

As soon as Kathy walked through her door at home and looked up at the clock, horrified to find that the time was actually 12:30, the watch on her wrist—whose hands had been frozen in the 11:30 position—suddenly began ticking again, starting up on its own without any tinkering on her part.

It never stopped working again.

CHAPTER 2.

BLUCIFER'S REVENGE

Unsurprising, Denver International Airport (DIA) sees a lot of traffic, both on the ground and in the air: It's the fifth-busiest airport in the United States, and the fifteenth in the entire world. Commercial aircraft both large and small stack up in the skies above DIA at all hours of the day and night.

At fifty-three square miles, it is also the biggest commercial airport in the US when measured in terms of sheer size, sprawling out to more than twice the size of Manhattan Island. Much has been made of the fact that DIA seems to have *much* more land than it could ever possibly use, even when taking potential future expansion into account. Some conspiracy theorists claim that the airport serves as a convenient cover for a secret underground complex that was built by (depending upon who one believes) either the United States government, or some shadowy New World Order cabal.

Others claim that a subterranean alien base can be found down there instead. They have nicknamed the airport "Area 52."

From the onset, conspiracy theories began to swirl around the fledgling Denver International Airport like moths drawn to a flame. Construction of the airport was late and the final costs came in at double the initially projected budget. Glitches in what was touted as a state-of-the-art automated luggage transportation system ultimately resulted in the system being shut down.

A Dead Creator

The main terminal is a distinctive-looking building and a familiar site to the hundreds of thousands of Coloradans who fly in and out of there each year. Its jagged white-pitched roof is deliberately intended to evoke memories of the Rocky Mountains. Passengers and their families have plenty of time to admire this incredible piece of architecture as they drive towards the airport on Peña Boulevard, but before long their eyes are drawn to something that looks far more sinister: the statue of a thirty-two foot high demonic blue mustang, which was sculpted rearing up majestically on its hind legs and watching over the airport with glowing red eyes.

Although its real name is *Blue Mustang*, locals have given the statue the rather less palatable moniker of *Blucifer*, a name that fits altogether too well with its malevolent appearance. Few of those who pass by the prancing creature are aware of its dark backstory, however. *Blucifer* holds the unsavory distinction of being one of the few pieces of art that has actually killed its creator.

Luis Jimenez was a respected and acclaimed artist from New Mexico, and *Blue Mustang* should have been his *piéce de resistance*. The fiberglass sculpture was huge and weighed in at a staggering 9,000 pounds when finally assembled. Tragically, Jimenez would not live to see it. *Mustang's* head was being moved across his studio via a hoist shortly after he had finished painting it in June of 2006. Although it is unclear exactly what happened next, control of the sculpture was somehow lost, causing it to swing free and slam into the unfortunate artist, pinning him against a steel girder and severing an artery in one of his legs. Although Jimenez was rushed to the nearby Lincoln County Medical Center, doctors were unable to save him, and he died of his injuries. He was sixty-five years old, and his loss is still keenly felt among members of the art community today.

This setback didn't stop his team from completing the structure, and it was then assembled, shipped to Denver, and finally set in place outside the airport in 2008. To say that *Blue Mustang* has been divisive would be an understatement: Local residents seem to either love it or hate it, and there has been at least one organized campaign to get rid of what some feel is a monstrosity and an eyesore. Inevitably, others have claimed that due to its role in the death of its creator, *Blue Mustang* (and by extension, the airport itself) is simply cursed.

Native American Singing

The curse story is fueled, in the finest Hollywood tradition, by local folklore, which claims that DIA was built on ancient Native American burial grounds. For many years now, passengers heading back to the main Jeppesen Terminal by way of Concourse "A" on foot have found themselves surrounded by the faint sounds of Native American singing and chanting when they hit the footbridge that crosses over the taxiway. The sounds are usually just at the edge of earshot, and are louder on some days than on others.

Some first-time visitors are taken by surprise, looking around in puzzlement in an attempt to locate the source of the chants. There is nothing supernatural about it, however: It is simply a part of the permanent DIA art setup, an attempt to express elements of local culture for visiting travelers, and it runs around the clock.

Despite the fact that little in the way of Native American graves have ever been unearthed in the area surrounding DIA, it hasn't stopped the stories of angry spirits haunting the airport from making the rounds.

Although Native American shamans carried out a ceremony of blessing when ground was broken on the facility back in the 1980s, what is less-commonly known is that a second ritual was performed eight years afterward. According to a 1995 *Westworld* article by Arthur Hodges entitled "Political Séance," the then-mayor of Denver, Wellington Webb, felt the need to establish a "DIA Spiritual Resolution Committee" to address the claims of long-dead Native Americans haunting the new airport construction project. This culminated in a number of Cheyenne and Arapaho tribal holy men traveling out to the DIA site and attempting to placate the restless souls of their long-dead ancestors in a nighttime ceremony. This was done secretly, and even today, specific details of the ceremony are kept under wraps.

Artworks

One of the first things that will strike the sharp-eyed observer when walking inside the Jeppesen Terminal is the artwork. Usually, paintings inside airport terminals are either nondescript works of art, or perhaps aviation themed. Not so at DIA, where newcomers often stop slack-jawed in front of a huge mural that would look more at home in a chamber of horrors than an international airport.

A soldier wearing a long green greatcoat and with his face covered by a gas mask is the centerpiece, clutching a bayonet-tipped assault rifle in one hand; with the other hand, he is skewering the white dove of peace on the point of a scimitar blade. Watching this horrific specter go down is a long line of wailing refugees, while three young children sleep in the rubble and ruins of bombed-out buildings. It is, to say the least, a cataclysmic sight for the traveler who is passing through DIA.

A companion piece shows a multi-ethnic gathering of children, huddled together and obviously very upset, while a forest burns heavily in the background. It is a cry against the pillage of the natural environment, according to the man who painted it.

Some members of the UFO and conspiracy theory communities have claimed that the tunnels underneath DIA contain thousands of human slaves, working under the auspices of Reptilian alien beings, and that the murals in the airport above are a direct reflection of that.

"The conspiracy theorists have interpreted it in the most naïve way," artist Leo Tanguma said during an interview with *Zing Magazine*, when asked about the subtext behind his DIA artwork. Nevertheless, many still believe that the paintings support the notion of a secret underground base.

Wander around the baggage area with a careful eye, and you will also catch sight of several gargoyles, sitting comfortably in open suitcases and sticking their tongues out at you. More than a few visitors have remarked upon the seemingly occult and antiquated nature of this particular type of statuary in a twenty-first-century airport made of glass and steel.

One traveler emailed the website *phantomsandmonsters.com* to tell of their own strange encounter with a statue within the halls of DIA. Passing through the nearly-deserted airport at one-thirty in the morning, the visitor claims to have stepped off one of the underground shuttles and headed out in search of a restroom, and caught sight of "a weird, very tall 'sculpture'—kind of like a dinosaur, but with alligator skin and a lizard face with BIG eyes."

Pausing to answer a phone call, the traveler turned away for a moment. When they turned back, the 'sculpture' had disappeared. This eyewitness is convinced that what they had encountered early that morning was in fact a Reptilian.

A Death

All of which brings us to the strange life and the sad (and some say suspicious) death of a man named Philip Schneider. When police officers entered Schneider's Oregon apartment in January 1996, they found Schneider's dead body. Although first reports asserted that he had died of a stroke or a heart attack roughly one week before his discovery, it would not be long before rumors began to circulate of Schneider having been strangled to death by an unknown assailant—with a length of rubber tubing wrapped three times around his neck (other accounts claim that it was piano wire).

Schneider told all who would listen that he had worked for the United States military as a structural engineer, helping to excavate underground installations. The reason put forward for his so-called murder was that he had become something of a whistleblower on the subject of secret alien bases, and he claimed to have dodged multiple attempts on his life over the years since he had first began to talk about his extraterrestrial experiences.

He maintained that in 1954, President Dwight Eisenhower signed a treaty with an extraterrestrial species that granted them permission to abduct and carry out biological tests on both cows and human beings. One of the underground bases that Schneider claimed to have helped build is located at Dulce, New Mexico, and was the scene of what is known in ufology circles as "The Dulce Firefight." Dulce is right on the Colorado border, and we will look at that case elsewhere in this book.

According to Schneider, he found himself in a cavern full of alien Greys when working on the Dulce base in 1979, and killed two of them after opening fire. The exchange of fire that ensued was said to have killed nearly seventy people. He also claimed to have gotten shot in the chest with some kind of alien energy weapon, which he said burned a hole in his body and subsequently gave him cancer. He maintained that he had stumbled upon a secret alien base at Dulce while helping excavate something similar for the US government.

It is not difficult to see why Phil Schneider gained something of a reputation for embellishing stories during his time as a speaker on the UFO circuit, and his accounts remain controversial among members of the UFO community today. What is his connection with the Denver International Airport, you may ask?

Schneider made some intriguing claims about the activity that was supposedly taking place beneath DIA. It is well-known that there is an extensive tunnel system beneath the airport, some of which houses the shuttle system that transports passengers between gates. Other sections can be explained away as being part of the now-defunct automated baggage transfer system. Shortly before his death, Phil Schneider maintained that he was able to gain access to the tunnel system in person and that these tunnels were connected to clandestine entrances to an underground base complex that was almost ninety square miles in size, a bustling subterranean undercity that went some eight levels deep.

Others have claimed that DIA is connected by underground tunnel networks to Cheyenne Mountain (home of NORAD—the North American Air Defense Command) and to the US Air Force academy in Colorado Springs. David Icke, the author and speaker whose theories are weighted very heavily toward extra-terrestrials and inter-dimensional beings being key components of a global conspiracy, cites Denver and its airport as being the headquarters of a forthcoming New World Order. A global catastrophe, which was believed by many to be taking place in 2012, was given as the time at which this world government would take over. As we all know, 2012 came and went with more of a whimper than a bang, and yet the conspiracy theories still persist.

It cannot be said that the staff of DIA's Global Communications and Marketing Division don't have a sense of humor: In 2015, a private link to a "secret" web page was posted (ostensibly by accident) on the airport's main website.

Current visitors to www.flydenver.com/newworldorder are greeted with a message that states: *Access Denied. You are not authorized to access this page.* When it was first released, however, the page portrayed itself as "a private site for our elite New World Order passengers, who value privacy and exclusivity." Images of the tunnels beneath the airport were accompanied by descriptions of a train that traveled directly to NORAD, underground sleeping quarters being built at the airport hotel, which was currently under construction, and a buried command bunker.

"OFFICIAL STATEMENT ON LEAKED WEBSITE:" began the press release. "Earlier this morning, a private link to a web page on the official Denver International Airport website, flydenver.com, was leaked by an unknown party to members of the media. At this time, our information technology team is working to secure the page, which was not intended for public distribution. While the airport certainly does offer world-class passenger amenities, with connections to more than 170 destinations around the world, the contents of this specific site were intended only for a select group of individuals with the proper security clearance."

One is forced to wonder how many people read this with increasing amazement and shock . . . until they realized that the link was released on April Fool's Day.

Then again, one is forced to wonder—if there really *is* a hidden base underneath DIA, and the whole thing has been one big smokescreen . . . just who exactly are the *real* fools?

CHAPTER 3.

SHEER "LOONACY"

Nestled in the heart of Summit County, the town of Breckenridge is well-known for its skiing, but other outdoor pursuits such as fishing and trail hiking also help to make it an extremely popular destination for vacationers all year round.

Breckenridge is policed by patrol officers of the Breckenridge Police Department and also by deputies of Summit County Sheriff's Office (SCSO). On the morning of October 3, 2014, the 911 emergency dispatchers began to receive calls of something unusual flying in the skies over the town. One call might have been dismissed as a hoax or a case of mistaken identity, but when reports came in from multiple citizens, the department decided that it had to investigate.

According to the many local people who observed them, a list that includes law enforcement officials and journalists, the shiny white objects assumed various formations against the clear blue mountain sky, including triangles and straight lines. There was minimal wind and barely a cloud in the sky.

Reporting live from Breckenridge for KUSA Denver's 9News, reporter Matt Renoux found no shortage of eyewitnesses to the mysterious aerial phenomena, though none of them—including investigating officers from Breckenridge PD or SCSO—were willing to appear before the cameras to share their testimony. SCSO spokesperson Taneil Ilano admitted that quite frankly, her department had "no clue" what the lights were. This soon became a moot point, however, as Renoux very quickly joined the ranks of observers himself.

In his news report, Renoux described seeing a series of three white dots hovering in the skies over Breckenridge earlier in the day, and the news station rolled footage of the objects their camera crew had captured, showing a small white object that was hovering in mid-air, effortlessly keeping station against the backdrop of the nearby mountains.

When asked whether they could have been drones, which has become a common explanation when attempting to debunk UFO sightings of late, Renoux discounted the possibility. "At times they would just sit there," the reporter explained, "for five or ten minutes, *fifteen* minutes, without moving an inch on the viewscreen in our camera, and then you would see a flash of light and they would take off across the edge of the mountain ridge behind me . . . *truly* unidentified flying objects in the skies above Breckenridge today . . ."

Several photographs of the UFOs were submitted to 9News by viewers, and the news station subsequently posted them in a gallery on its website. They all showed a similar-looking object, poorly-defined but apparently spherical in appearance, standing out in stark contrast against either the blue sky or mountain range behind it. Whatever material the object is composed of, it appears to be highly reflective, just as eyewitnesses have described.

By one o'clock in the afternoon, the UFOs had disappeared.

The Federal Aviation Administration (FAA) chose not to comment upon the many sightings, so it was left to the military to provide an official position. Speaking on behalf of NORAD, the men and women who keep a watchful eye on US airspace around the clock, Major Beth Smith stated that, "NORAD is not tracking any anomalies in that location. We are investigating." The results of that investigation do not appear to have been made public at the time of writing, although it would be worth noting that this incident would be far from the first time that UFOs have appeared to be invisible to radar.

Of course, it goes without saying that if the object (or objects) happened to be secret aircraft being operated by the United States government, NORAD would hardly admit to having tracked them either, even if they were fully aware of their existence and nature.

So is it possible that the UFOs were a classified, experimental US Air Force flight?

The National UFO Reporting Center (NUFORC) logged a sighting report for the Breckenridge incident on October 3, at 11:58 a.m. Peter

Davenport, the director of NUFORC, commented that the UFO sighting may have been explainable as a number of helium-filled balloons, operating at high altitude, but then goes on to caution the reader that such balloons are usually seen alone. If balloons are the answer to the Breckenridge mystery, there would have to be at least three, all of which were capable of changing formation from a triangle into a straight line, holding a stationary position in mid-air, and then shooting off at high speed—something which is extremely un-balloon-like behavior.

Nor were the sightings restricted to the area around Breckenridge; they were seen much further afield, some as far away as the neighboring state of Utah. The day before, October 2, the Mutual UFO Network (MUFON) recorded a sighting in the City of Taylorsville, in which three extremely reflective solid objects hovered in mid-air for approximately half an hour, before moving slowly off in a southwesterly direction. The UFOs were in a straight line, but echeloned at what the five eyewitnesses thought was a forty-five-degree angle, finally breaking formation as they passed out of sight.

According to that same MUFON report, military fighter jets buzzed the UFOs on several occasions, making several passes as though keeping a watchful eye on them but unwilling to get too close. Similar sighting reports flooded in from across Utah, most of them describing essentially the same thing—unidentified flying objects that were extremely similar to those that would be seen over Breckenridge the next day.

Fox 13 News, broadcasting out of Salt Lake City, was also bombarded with phone calls from concerned viewers who were reporting formations of white objects that were seen high up in the sky.

With so many witnesses observing such similar UFO activity, we must ask ourselves whether there is a simple explanation for whatever it was that they were seeing. The balloon possibility is given credence by the behavior of a rather unlikely source: Google's Project *Loon*.

The giant multinational corporation embarked upon Project *Loon* in 2013. *Loon* is a remarkable and audacious concept: It is intended to use a network of robust, high-altitude stratospheric balloons to deliver Internet connectivity to the two-thirds of our world that currently lacks it. No matter how remote a location may be, Project *Loon* balloons could easily drift into position above it and allow anybody living there to connect to the World Wide Web.

Made of polyethylene plastic, the *Loon* balloons measure about fifty feet (some fifteen meters) wide and twelve meters high when they are fully inflated with helium gas, and also happen to reflect the sunlight very effectively indeed.

A little more than two weeks before the Breckenridge incident, a Project *Loon* balloon caused quite a stir as it drifted through the skies high above the Colorado City of Longmont. Cruising at well over 60,000 feet, the *Loon* balloon was mistaken for a UFO by more than a few citizens, who rushed to report their sightings to the local newspaper and authorities. Some observers remarked on how spherical the object was, with some mistaking it for a very bright star in the early evening sky.

In an article published in the Longmont-based *Daily Camera* newspaper, reporter Joe Rubino revealed that "Google officials on Tuesday confirmed a few *Loon* balloons were in the Colorado area on Monday as part of ongoing program testing based in California, but declined to say how many of them might have been near Longmont."

The phrasing is interesting, particularly "*a few Loon* balloons," because it confirms that the stratospheric balloons can indeed travel in packs, for want of a better term. Therefore, it is not unreasonable to conjecture that a string of three *Loons* would be what was sighted over Utah on October 2, and Breckenridge on October 3.

At this point in the story, some will have already shrugged their shoulders and said to themselves "case closed!" It is certainly tempting do so. After all, we have an apparent smoking gun on our hands here: a conveniently mundane explanation that involves high-altitude reflective balloons, putting a slightly fresh veneer on an old warhorse that has been trotted out time and time again to explain UFO sightings ever since the Roswell incident of 1947, in the form of the crashed weather balloon that was paraded in front of reporters along with a somewhat embarrassed Major Jesse Marcel Jr.

However, there are one or two nagging questions with the Project *Loon* theory, as it relates to the Breckenridge sighting, which we must try to answer. While we do know that there were several *Loon* balloons in the skies above Utah on October 2, it is not known precisely how many there were, and whether they moved through the same vicinity in which the eyewitnesses lived. Nonetheless, this does increase the likelihood that a *Loon* was responsible for some, if not all, of the sightings.

Secondly, if there truly was such an innocuous, everyday explanation, why did the FAA fail to mention it when they were contacted by the media, choosing instead to refer them to the National UFO Reporting Center? Such a simple reason would look much less suspicious than the usual "no comment" or blanket denials that some federal agencies choose to employ.

Thirdly, while the behavior of the UFOs initially seems to match with that of a balloon, consider Matt Renoux's description: "At times they would just sit there, for five or ten minutes, fifteen minutes, without moving an inch on the viewscreen in our camera," their behavior suddenly changed drastically. ". . . then you would see a flash of light and they would take off across the edge of the mountain ridge," the seasoned reporter concluded. While the flash of light might conceivably be the balloon changing its aspect in relation to the observer and catching the rays of the sun from a different angle, balloons do not usually take off at high speed.

Could a sudden gust of wind explain this sudden rapid exit, however? I believe that this is entirely possible too, particularly considering the fact that the *Loons* are designed to essentially surf the air currents within the upper atmosphere, using sophisticated computer algorithms to predict how best to catch the next "wave" of air and ride it to their desired destination.

So, all in all, it seems as though the makers of the world's most popular search engine are to blame for several hundred UFO sightings in the fall of 2014, but there is one further fly in the ointment before we can say so for sure. When considering the flight behavior of these particular UFOs, we must return to Boulder County once more in order to consider the testimony of another eyewitness.

Cammeren Young of Denver saw what he believes to be the same UFO early that same morning of October 3, while driving west on Highway 52 in the area of Longmont. It was approximately 7:45 a.m., and Cammeren caught sight of something that would make his jaw drop in astonishment: There in the skies above him was a shiny triangular shape that seemed to be paralleling the highway. "It almost looked like chrome to me," says the thirty-nine-year-old. There were no lights visible at all on the object that he saw, unlike some of the other reports, but he remains convinced that it was the same UFO that hovered over the Town of Breckenridge.

The object that Cammeren saw appeared to be spinning, rotating about a central axis. Although he doesn't feel confident enough to judge its rate of speed, the object was moving extremely quickly—far too quickly, he claims, for it to have been a drone, a helicopter, or even a conventional aircraft . . . or a high-altitude balloon.

"In my opinion," Cammeren declares firmly, "Man did not create the object that I saw."

Did Cammeren also witness one of the *Loons,* catching the early morning sunlight as it rose above the Rocky Mountains, or did he see something else? Neither he, nor we, will ever know for sure.

CHAPTER 4.
ABDUCTED

I have known Al (not his real name) for several years now. We met through the course of our work and share a mutual drive for helping to educate the next generation of EMTs and paramedics, born out of a lengthy career in the fire service for both of us.

Although he does not shout it from the rooftops or mention it in casual conversation, Al belongs to that remarkable class of human beings known as alien abductees. My interest in all things paranormal is something that I have never bothered to conceal, particularly once my books on the subject began to be published, but it was only when the opportunity arose for me to write on the subject of UFOs—the book that you are now holding in your hands—that I approached Al with a genuine sense of curiosity about his experiences.

What I found was rather unexpected, to say the least, and more than a little worrying. Al's story would turn out to be remarkable and bears a sinister slant that will resonate with some readers, while disturbing others.

I first approached Al after a break between lessons at the academic institution where we both teach. Closing the classroom door quietly behind me, I hesitantly asked him whether he would consent to an interview for an upcoming book on UFOs that I was working on.

Al closed his eyes for a moment to think about it.

"Are you sure you're ready to enter this world?" he asked me calmly, giving me a pointed no-BS look. "Because if you do your research, you'll find that for a lot of people, once you start taking an interest in them"—

he did not dignify "them" with a name—"then they start taking an interest in you. They call it *high strangeness*."

I had heard the term before, in passing. Dr. J. Allen Hynek is credited with originating the concept during an assembly of the United Nations in 1978:

- Mr. Chairman, there exists today a world-wide phenomenon . . . indeed if it were not world-wide I should not be addressing you and these representatives from many parts of the world. There exists a global phenomenon the scope and extent of which is not generally recognized. It is a phenomenon so strange and foreign to our daily terrestrial mode of thought that it is frequently met by ridicule and derision by persons and organizations unacquainted with the facts. [. . .]
- I refer, of course, to the phenomenon of UFOs . . .

Being a qualified astronomer and consultant on many of the official US Government-led studies of the UFO phenomenon, such as Projects Sign, Grudge, and finally the infamous Project Blue Book, Hynek knew whereof he spoke. Steven Spielberg used Hynek's "Close Encounter" method of categorizing the different levels of UFO contact to great effect in his movie *Close Encounters of the Third Kind.*

High Strangeness is still commonly used throughout the UFO community as a measure of just how many weird and bizarre occurrences surround a specific encounter with the unknown. The greater the number of inexplicable data points confront the perplexed investigator, the higher the level of strangeness it is said to be.

A case in point: I live not too far from the Denver International Airport. If I look out toward the eastern horizon on pretty much any night of the year, I can see bright lights in the sky—that's the DIA traffic pattern, aircraft stacked up and waiting to land. Imagine that one of those bright lights begins to move toward me, breaking the pattern and making a bee-line straight for where I'm standing. It then turns into a series of smaller lights with different colors. At this point, we're still talking Low Strangeness: After all, it could simply be a case of an aircraft breaking the pattern, moving in a direction that happens to coincide with my position, and then turning away, showing me the lights of the tail and the tip of each wing (the brighter white landing light dims significantly when the aircraft turns away). All well and good: This isn't too hard to explain, and the likelihood of this being a simple case of an aircraft doing its own thing is one that most people would be very comfortable with.

But now let's say that as the light comes toward my position, it doesn't change aspect. Instead, the white light grows brighter and brighter, playing a beam along the ground in front of it. Nobody else but me seems to be aware of its presence. As the source of the light draws nearer to me, the light grows larger, brighter, and more intense; when it's no more than, say, a hundred feet away, I can begin to make out a saucer-shaped craft behind the glare of the spotlight. Round windows can dimly be made out, with inverted teardrop-shaped gray heads peering out through them. There's a flash of white light as the beam finally hits me, and then . . . nothing. I come back to consciousness four hours later (my watch has stopped at exactly the time that the beam struck) in my own bed, with no recollection of what happened to me.

That, my friends, is High Strangeness. There are just too many bizarre and inexplicable factors at work to be brushed aside as "swamp gas," the planet Venus, hallucinations, or a plain and simply vivid imagination. Hynek puts it in more scientific and precise terms, defining High Strangeness as "a measure of the number of information bits the report contains, each of which is difficult to explain in common-sense terms."

It would have been easy to brush off Al's warning with a smile. As a paranormal investigator for the past twenty years, however, I'd seen examples of what he was talking about on far too many occasions. "When you take an interest in ghosts," an old mentor of mine once warned me in exactly the same way, "they sometimes take an interest in you right back. Are you sure that's what you want?" Well, yes—I had been sure, and although I had spent a fulfilling couple of decades investigating claims of ghosts and haunted houses, it had resulted in my having brought something home with me: a something that only went away after my house had been blessed from top to bottom by a friendly Catholic priest of my acquaintance. Shadowy figures had been seen around the home by both my wife and I; a number of framed pictures had been pushed off the mantelpiece, narrowly avoiding our slumbering cat, Vlad, who used up one of his nine lives in getting out of the way; and a woman's voice was heard coming from somewhere downstairs, causing my beloved dog,

Greta, to go tearing downstairs with her hackles raised, only to launch a bark-attack at what turned out to be nothing but thin air.

Was I ready for that level of strangeness to invade my home life once more?

This time, I was the one who needed to close his eyes and think for a minute. I let out a long, slow breath.

"Yes," I told Al. "I'm sure. Let's do this."

We arranged a time and a place to meet. Al favored a restaurant that was roughly halfway between our two homes, and after a busy day at work, I sat down with him to eat some truly mouth-watering bison and let the digital voice recorder sitting on the tabletop between us take down every fact and facet of Al's extraordinary story.

In advance of the interview, Al had prepared an extensive dossier of his memories concerning his UFO experiences. Times, dates, places, and other pertinent information was all recorded and annotated in a notebook, interspersed with sketches of the various craft that he had seen during his encounters. For the next three hours, Al would speak to me of his experiences in a clear, calm, steady voice, pausing only to answer one of my questions or to clarify some key point.

As Al talked, there were times when his eyes filled with tears of genuine sorrow, particularly when he spoke of his daughters; at others, Al had to stop and gather his thoughts, as he could feel or hear "them" telling him to stop talking, because "other people aren't supposed to know about this, we aren't supposed to talk about it." When this happened, Al would close his eyes, pause for a moment, and then resume speaking, as though pushing through some form of intense resistance.

"I have an alien daughter," he explained during one such interlude. "After I spoke to you, and agreed to be interviewed for your book, all three versions of her came to me . . . and all three said the same thing. The little one said, 'Shhhh! Daddy, you know we're not supposed to talk about this.' The fourteen year-old said, 'Dad, we're not supposed to tell!' And the eldest, she's thirty-five or thirty-six, said 'Dad, you know we're not supposed to discuss this—ever.'"

I have no doubt that some will choose to dismiss Al's remarkable story as being a product of his imagination, a delusion, or perhaps some form of behavioral disorder, such as schizophrenia. In answer to that, I can simply state that having interviewed him at length, Al most certainly believes with every fiber of his being that the remarkable events he related to me are real, and actually took place. He is certainly not out to deceive anybody. Nor is he in it for fame, publicity, or money; he has not been paid one cent to relate his story, and he insisted that I change his name prior to publication in order that he might remain anonymous. Needless to say, these are not the actions of an attention-seeker or publicity hound.

Al does not have a documented history of mental illness, and has worked for many years as a first responder in the emergency services. Were he truly schizophrenic or suffering from some similar mental malady, it would almost certainly have been detected by his colleagues and ultimately have resulted in his dismissal from the service.

His story is by turns remarkable, unbelievable, tragic, exciting, and sometimes simply head-scratching, but if one studies the UFO phenomenon and that subset which includes alien abduction, one thing becomes very, very clear: Al is not alone.

Friends? Not Really

"I call them my 'friends,'" Al told me, interlacing his hands carefully and resting them on the tabletop. "They've been with me for most of my life . . . and they're not really friends at all."

Al has a younger sister and a brother who is six years his senior. His story really begins at the age of three, when the family was enjoying a sunny day out at Waterton Canyon, not too far outside Denver. Some six miles long, the canyon is a very popular hiking, biking, and horseback-riding location for families and day-trippers, particularly due to the proximity of the South Platte River. The family had found a deserted stretch of stream and settled down to enjoy themselves.

Al's brother was balancing up on a rock, just playing around as boys will; his younger sister was tossing small stones into the water, enjoying the splish-splash each one made as it skimmed, his stepfather was trying his hand at fishing,and his mother was sitting on a rock, smoking a cigarette and engrossed in a novel.

"Cut it out," Al's stepfather hollered at his little sister, clearly annoyed. "Quit throwing rocks. You'll scare the fish!"

Three-year-old Al was bored out of his mind. The outdoors wasn't remotely fun for him. He would rather have been home playing with his toys.

And then everything changed, just like that.

Suddenly, Al's mother was running toward him as fast as her legs could carry her. The book she had been reading was discarded, instantly forgotten, along with her cigarette. A look of true fear was plastered across her face. Without breaking her stride for even a second, she scooped up her daughter and tucked her under one arm. Then it was Al's turn, as his mother ran full-tilt in his direction, reaching out for him with her free arm.

Al's stepfather had a hard and fast rule about his most treasured fishing rod: It must never, ever be allowed to touch the water, not for a moment and not even a little bit of it. Except that now, he had dropped the prized rod from one slackly dangling arm, allowing the final third of it to trail off under the surface of the water. That he might do such a thing was simply inconceivable. His eyes stared away incredulously at something beyond young Al's line of sight.

The young Al hadn't the faintest idea of what was going on. Following his mother's gaze, he turned to get a better look at what had frightened her so. Then he understood why she had suddenly become so desperately afraid.

His elder brother was frozen into immobility, arms held out by his sides, and wearing the same look of slack-jawed incredulity that his parents had. What made this even more terrifying for the young Al was the fact that his brother was somehow floating in the air above the rock, his feet no longer making contact with its surface . . . and there, in the sky behind him, was the UFO.

It was a flying disk some forty feet in diameter, if Al's memory serves him right. The heads of alien beings could plainly be seen peering out at him from a single band of glass windows that reminded him of the band running around a hat. The creatures were the classic Greys, and regarded the boy coldly with almond-shaped black eyes.

As if that were not incredible enough, above the first flying disk was a second, offset to the rear a little in the same way that military fighter pilots fly with wingmen, in order to cover their six o'clock position from surprise attack by enemy fighters. The closest was at an altitude of twenty-five feet, and its wingman just below the level of the trees. Both disks were a metallic silver in color.

Time seemed to unfreeze for a moment. With her legs and heart pounding furiously, Al's mother somehow managed to reach the safety of their car; yet it would turn out to be an illusory sanctuary at best. Throwing Al and his sister into the back seat, she tuned out the screaming and crying children as best she could, reaching into the glove box to retrieve her trusty .38 revolver. Pivoting on her feet, she aimed the pistol in the direction of the two stacked saucers with trembling hands, standing guard between them and her two youngest children.

His curiosity getting the better of his fear, Al climbed up onto his knees, determined to get a good look out of the car's back window.

"Then everything suddenly went white," he told me, shaking his head, "and the next thing I know, we're all five of us driving back down the canyon like nothing ever happened."

"Well, we didn't get any fish, so we're gonna stop and get hamburgers," Al's stepdad announced, guiding the car carefully around a bend in the road.

Al's brother and sister were on either side of him in the back seat, which was an odd placement for the three children: Al's baby sister always sat in between her parents in the front of the car. His mother insisted on it, so that she could throw out an arm and protect her in the event of a crash (she figured that the boys could brace themselves). However it was that they had gotten in the car—it felt somehow . . .wrong.

To make things even stranger, none of them had any recollection of what had happened following their encounter with the two flying disks.

For years, this memory remained buried in the depths of Al's mind, locked away out of sight. It took a past-life regression during his twenties to dislodge it, causing it to rise back to the surface once more.

"I know that I was taken on board one of those ships," Al explained, "but as to what happened inside there—I got nothing. After the regression, I did my best not to think about it . . . and I was pretty successful, until I did a rescue training up at that same stretch of the canyon a few years later, and damn near came unglued. All the memories came flooding back, but I still have no recollection of what happened after the white light hit."

The family returned to their home and resumed the business of everyday life. Al's fourth birthday came and went . . . and so did the Greys. The intruders were no respecters of the clock, and came into his bedroom at all hours of the day and night. Sometimes they would step out of his closet; at other times, they would materialize at the window and pass through it without taking the trouble to open it first.

Nor were the visitations restricted to his bedroom, sometimes taking place when he was outdoors playing. Al always knew when he was due for an impending encounter. Seizure sufferers become used to the sensation known as an aura; this may be a series of flashing lights or images, a distinct smell or unusual noise. Sometimes it is nothing more than a distinct feeling that a seizure is imminent. The exact nature of the aura depends upon the part of the brain in which the seizure originates.

Al developed a similar sensation prior to a visit from the Greys. He would feel a sort of vibration—"like a sound, but it's not a sound," as he describes it—that served as an early warning system. Al believes that what he experienced was a vibration that was somehow attuned to and harmonized with his body. It guaranteed that within no more than a few hours, he would be abducted by the creatures yet again. There was no point running, because there was nowhere on Earth that he could hide from them.

Al still has no knowledge of what occurred to him during those many abductions. After experiencing the signature vibration, the Greys would visit, take him away . . . and then suddenly, he would find himself returned to his room, with no recollection of the past few hours. Nor did anybody ever seem to miss him.

One particularly disturbing visitation occurred late one night when he was six years old. Al and his brother were hanging out in their room, when he suddenly felt the usual vibration telling him that they were coming. Sure enough, a few minutes later, one stepped out of the closet. It smelled like wet cardboard, and on closer inspection, its skin looked like more of a mottled pale yellow color than gray. Dashing out into the corridor, Al could see a second creature: This one was larger than the first, unusually so, and blocked off any possible escape route that he may have tried to take. It came into the boys' bedroom through the door.

Al's brother had completely shut down, not moving or acknowledging the incredible events that were playing out in the confines of the small bedroom. Al still wanted to make a dash for the comfort and security of his mother, but was cut off. Both creatures closed in on him, backing the boy into a corner. He screamed for all that he was worth, but no help came. One of the Greys suddenly reached out and poked him in the ribs with a stick. The stick was roughly two feet long, and the end of it glowed a hot red, like the tip of a poker just taken from the fireplace. A wave of nausea came over him at the implement's touch, making him double over and vomit. Using the stick like a cattle prod, the entity forced the still-nauseated Al back into bed. Once they were satisfied that he and his brother were both in their beds, they both retreated stealthily into the hallway outside the room.

Footsteps sounded out in the hallway. Not the light footfalls of the intruders, Al knew, because he recognized the sound of his mother's footsteps approaching his room. Peering through the doorway, he watched as the stick-wielder jabbed it into his mother's side, in exactly the same spot, beneath her left arm. She swatted at the stick, but missed. Unlike her son, Al's mother was not overcome with nausea. She burst into the boys' bedroom and took Al into her arms, telling him that everything was going to be all right.

"She was still half-asleep," Al recalled some forty years later. "She kept saying that it was just a dream, just a nightmare, but I knew that it wasn't . . ."

Both creatures then stepped back into the darkness of the hallway outside the boys' bedroom, disappearing silently into the shadows. Al believes that the bizarre episode was an experiment, intended to see whether they could provoke a nurturing response from his mother, testing whether the bond between them was such that she would protect him when both of them were sick and hurt. If this is indeed the case, then it would appear that the experiment was a success. It's interesting to note, however, that Al's brother was completely ignored during the entire experience, as though he was nothing more than an extraneous variable.

The visitations and subsequent abductions continued, settling into an almost rhythmic cycle: every ninety days, almost as regular as clockwork, Al would experience the vibration and the visitors would return. Speaking of clockwork, after each experience, his mother would have to go to Woolworths in order to buy a new watch: Something about the abductions caused hers to break every single time.

These contacts persisted off and on until Al turned twelve or thirteen. Where was he being taken during each abduction episode?

"Aboard a ship, along with a bunch of other children of all ages—maybe twenty or thirty children in all. We're being told how great this is all going to be." Al describes the interior of the ship as being dimly backlit and divided up into several rooms. No matter how afraid he was during each abduction, Al also experienced a powerful sense of his being meant to be there—that some ineffable purpose lay behind it all, a grand scheme to whose details he was not privy.

Car Camping Gone Wrong

The family was a big fan of what they liked to call "car camping," packing a picnic lunch and driving out to some remote and picturesque spot on the weekend in order to enjoy it. When Al was ten, he experienced one such car camp that he would never forget, out in the woods to the south of Morrison, not far from Highway 285.

Like most brothers, Al and his brother Bobby were healthily competitive, which is why the afternoon found the two boys racing one another up a rocky slope, straining hard to be the first one to reach the top. Struggling for purchase and wanting to gain a little extra leverage, Al reached out and grabbed what he thought at first was a five-inch tree stump . . .

. . . only to have it reach out and grab him back.

Al was lifted high into the air. He tried to scream, opened his mouth wide, but no sound came out. Looking to his left, he could see that his brother was also being held captive, and was dangling by his feet. Although the classic *Star Trek* episode titled "Arena" would not air until January 1967 (several years into the future), Al maintains that the creatures that held him and his brother captive were almost identical to the reptilian alien race known as the Gorn.

The two big reptilians moved quickly through the forest, still holding their captives in one hand (or claw). Suddenly, the creatures stopped, dumping the boys unceremoniously to the ground. The reptilians appeared to communicate telepathically; although Al could hear them speak, their mouths did not move, and he realized that he was not "hearing" in a conventional sense.

"Put them back," rumbled the one that seemed to be the leader. "They're marked." .

Al blacked out.

When he came to, he was sitting on the edge of the rock face, with a forty-foot drop below him. He cried out in surprise, afraid as much of the steep drop below him as he was of what had just happened to them. Looking to his right, Al saw Bobby similarly positioned a few feet away. The two boys carefully made their way to safety.

Once they were alone again, Al asked Bobby, "What the heck was that?"

"Don't ever talk about it again," Bobby replied in a hushed whisper. "We're not supposed to talk about it."

If one theme runs consistently through Al's story, it's that none of this is supposed to be spoken of—or discussed—with anybody else. I asked him why there was such a veil of secrecy in place over the abduction phenomenon, hoping to gain an insider's perspective of it all.

"I don't know," he admits candidly, then goes on to speak of there being multiple extraterrestrial races involved in the phenomenon, all of whom have their own unique and separate agenda.

High School Strangeness

The year was 1973, and Al was out driving one night with a bunch of friends from high school. They were cruising in an isolated part of Arapahoe County, close to what would eventually become the City of Centennial in 2001.

At first, nobody thought much of the fact that there was a light visible from a little further ahead up the road; but as they closed in on it, every jaw in the car dropped when they saw that a small vessel—what Al terms a "scout ship"—had landed off to the side of the road. The underside of the craft glowed an angry red-orange, as though it had just entered Earth's atmosphere at high speed.

Unlike the classic saucer-shaped UFOs that he had encountered before, this particular craft bore a triangular shape; it is interesting to note that triangular UFOs did not gain prominence until the so-called "Belgian UFO Wave" that ran from 1989 through 1990. As their car sped by it, all four of its occupants turning incredulously to stare at what could only be a spacecraft of extraterrestrial origin, the wedge rose smoothly into the air and turned to chase them down the long dirt road.

Flooring the accelerator, Al managed to get the car up to around one hundred mph, no mean feat on such a bumpy surface. When they began to hit the main roads, the craft soared higher into the sky behind them, but stuck doggedly to their tail all the way into Denver. It's fascinating to note that while Al and his companions could all see the craft quite distinctly, none of the other cars on the road reacted to its presence at all.

Unsure of where exactly to go with a UFO tailing them, Al and his friends rejected the idea of a police station and instead opted to go to the closest radio station instead. Grabbing the doorman excitedly, they pointed out the UFO.

"That? That's just three stars," the man said, apparently bored—and completely ignoring the fact that the "three stars" were moving.

"*The hell it is!*" Al replied in frustration. "Those three stars followed us here!"

Al and his friends waited anxiously at the radio station until the craft seemed to lose interest and disappeared. Needless to say, they never wanted to go out for a drive with him again after that.

Later that same year, Al was hanging out with an old high-school friend named Roger. Roger was aware of Al's past (as it related to High Strangeness) and was surprisingly cool with the whole idea. Driving along Speer Boulevard early one afternoon, Al checked his side-view mirror and was aghast to see the form of a man in a silver suit; behind the man was a classic saucer-shaped UFO. Frowning, he checked his rear-view mirror, and saw exactly the same thing. The man was extremely tall, and his head was completely bald.

Yet again, other drivers seemed oblivious of this bizarre phenomenon, which was taking place on a major metropolitan thoroughfare in broad daylight. "This was a projection," Al explains when queried: "a visual-auditory hallucination that was being transmitted directly into our minds. Like a hologram, if you will."

Roger had just flipped down the passenger-side visor and was in the process of combing his hair back, when he caught sight of the man and saucer that were being projected as well. He instantly froze, mouth agape in astonishment as his brain attempted to process just what it was that his eyes were showing him.

As the silver-suited man spoke, his words manifested inside Al's mind, telling him things that Al maintains have since come true. "You will care for the people that we need to have cared for," was one such statement, and Al believes that this referred to his future career choice: that of firefighter-paramedic.

The man and his craft disappeared as quickly as they had arrived. Pulling into the parking lot of a nearby high school, the two boys sat in silence for a moment. Finally, Roger said, "Did you see that shit in the mirror!?"

Al simply nodded slowly.

"Does that crap happen to you all of the time?"

It would be tempting to dismiss their experience as being nothing more than a hallucination, nothing more than the product of an over-active imagination. When the two boys compared notes afterward, however, it turned out that Roger had heard the same voice, speaking the very same words, inside his own head. Al would begin quoting a line spoken by the bald man, and Roger would finish the sentence—and vice versa. Although mass-hallucinations are a documented phenomenon, this would not happen to such a detailed and specific degree. This particular hallucination seemed targeted at the two boys. To this day, Al remains unsure of its purpose.

Past the Point

The abductions continued throughout Al's adult life, and each encounter left him with the uneasy sensation that he was being used as breeding stock. As their influence on his life increased, Al reacted in one of the least healthy ways possible: He chose to involve himself, by his own admission, very heavily in the drug scene.

"I took a lot of speed for a while, around 1974–75," he admits, shaking his head. "I pretty much lived on it. That way, I wouldn't sleep for hours or days, because when I slept, they were there."

It was a protracted effort to stay awake for long periods in order to discourage the visitors.

One day, Al was in Denver's Washington Park, sitting on a bench with a head in hands. He had taken a number of white cross pills (amphetamines) that day. Sleepless almost to the point of a nervous breakdown, he began to cry.

In the interests of balance, it must be noted that some common side-effects of long-term amphetamine abuse include schizophrenia-like psychosis, along with both visual and auditory hallucinations; Al is also very lucky not to have wound up dead, thanks to the severe strain that such drugs place on the cardiovascular system. As a well-educated paramedic, he was very aware of these risks—but so great was the misery inflicted upon him by the abductions and visitations that he was simply past the point of caring.

The drugs may have reduced the frequency of the abductions, but now he was beginning to hear the voices of his abductors speaking to him inside his own head.

"If you don't stop that, you can't help us," a woman's voice cautioned him disapprovingly. The voice was crystal-clear in his mind and caused a change in his feelings almost immediately. He felt as though he would be left out of something vitally important—some crucial but unseen bigger picture—if he continued to ravage his body with the drugs, something for which their biological pollution would render him unsuitable.

It took three weeks, but with grit and determination, Al was finally able to kick his drug habit, and has remained clean ever since.

Seeking a healthier way in which he could live with the phenomena that plagued him, Al sought therapy and counseling. His first counselor died of natural causes, and the second therapist he tried flatly refused to entertain the notion of UFOs or abduction, but the third seemed more open to the concept, and so Al decided to give him the benefit of the doubt. During his third session with this new counselor (whose name was Randy), Al was surprised to be given a written test and was instructed to fill it out.

"What's this?" Al asked suspiciously, turning the document over in his hands. It appeared to be a number of multiple-choice questions.

"Fill it out. It was mailed to me from a post office box in St. Louis, believe it or not. The cover letter said that I was to give it to anybody who claimed to be an abductee. So, here we are . . ."

Against his better instincts, Al sat down and took the test. When the last answer had been circled, Randy placed it carefully into the return envelope, sealed it, and mailed it off.

The following week, when Al returned for his counseling session, he found two Men in Black (MIB) waiting for him at his therapist's office. Each was at least six feet tall, weighed approximately 200 pounds, and wore a completely black suit with a white shirt bisected by a skinny black tie; each also had deathly pale skin, which looked distinctly inhuman to Al as he eyed them up suspiciously. He couldn't make out their eyes, as each was wearing a pair of expensive-looking shades.

"Why didn't you answer question 26?" demanded the first MIB.

"Because it's a test question," Al shot back, "a control question. If I'd have answered it, it would have made me look like a fake. And I ain't no fake."

Ignoring Al completely, the second MIB turned to address Randy. "Send us all his bills. We've got this. We'll cover everything."

From that point on, Al never had to pay for a single therapy session.

Shocking

In 1980, when Al was living in an apartment close to the intersection of Sheridan and Hampden, the abductions changed in nature once again.

Now Al was given a specific purpose: He was to learn to read and write the extraterrestrial language. Twenty-six letters were taught (though he admits that there may possibly have been more that were not) and he was required to study and then duplicate the alien characters with great precision: If the work was judged to be sloppy by his extraterrestrial tutors, he received an electric shock.

Overseeing Al's linguistic instruction was one of the "praying mantis"-type of creatures, which have been reported components of the abduction phenomenon since Reme Baca and Jose Padilla (two young boys from New Mexico) first claimed to encounter them during a 1945 UFO crash incident. The thing simply sat there, rhythmically moving its head from side to side, staring at him as it manipulated the controls of a high-tech desk with its pincers. By Al's estimate, the mantis had to have been at least eight feet tall, and it was triggering the electric shocks for each perceived infraction. Al would go to what some refer to as "night school" for much of his life, learning (the hard way) to read and write the extraterrestrial language flawlessly.

A Trip to Utah

High Strangeness continued to plague Al's life. In 1982, he recalls driving through Nevada during broad daylight while on a road trip, and suddenly experiencing the all too familiar vibration that signified an impending visit. The next thing Al knew, he was awakening the following day . . . in Utah, sitting in his parked car, without the faintest idea of how he had gotten there. This time, however, he does know what happened during that block of missing time.

"I was on a ship, along with people I knew. Some of them worked at my fire department. We were all brought together for a purpose."

Don't Talk!

Communion, Whitley Strieber's classic account of alien abduction, was published in 1987, and helped catapult the Grey aliens firmly into the forefront of the public consciousness. Although they had been spoken of and portrayed before (the entities featured at the conclusion of *Close Encounters of the Third Kind* bear a striking resemblance to them), it wasn't until Strieber's book that the creatures became instantly recognizable.

Communion can rightly be called a publishing phenomenon in its own right, and the soulless black, almond-shaped eyes of the Greys were soon staring back at browsers from every bookstore window in the United States.

Standing in front of one such bookstore, Al and his girlfriend stared right back. She asked him why he was frowning.

"The face is wrong. They didn't get the details quite right." Nevertheless, he recognized an approximation of the old, familiar abductors, and it sent a chill running along the length of his spine that he remembers to this day.

This was the same year in which Al was shown his daughter for the very first time, at the age of eighteen months. She is a human-alien hybrid, although he does not know the identity of her mother. As he talked of her, Al was visibly overcome with emotion. When I offered him the opportunity to take a minute or two, he shook his head vehemently.

"No," he told me firmly, eyes closed, "because I can hear them screaming."

"What are they screaming?"

"Don't talk. *DON'T TALK!*"

Al felt an instant connection with the tiny babe-in-arms, and knew instinctively that it was his the first time she was given to him to hold. It would not be the last he would see of her.

A year later, in 1988, Al had the terrifying experience of waking one night to find himself completely naked, more than one hundred feet up in the air. He was being drawn up into one of their ships, or perhaps more accurately "sucked in" as he prefers to put it. He was still screaming when he came inside, until one of the inhabitants reached out and touched him. The next thing he remembers he was waking up covered in dirt and leaves outside his home the next morning. He sensed that the creatures were not happy that he had awoken mid-flight, and thought that they might perhaps have been expressing that displeasure by returning him outdoors this time.

A few weeks later, Al ran into his former counselor, Randy, in a seemingly random encounter. "We don't have a doctor-patient relationship any more, and it would be great to catch up," Randy told him earnestly. "I'm having a get-together in a few days' time, and I'd love it if you could come."

Figuring "why not?" Al took his girlfriend, Diane, along with him to the party at Randy's place. Who should turn out to be there but Ken, the second counselor Al had tried to engage with during his early steps into therapy. The two men got to talking. Ken had a remarkable story to tell.

Some two weeks after dismissing Al and his "wild stories" of alien encounters, Ken had begun to experience something that was a cross between a dream and a vision on a regular basis. These experiences centered upon a mysterious woman. Finally caving in to the strange compulsion he was feeling, Ken flew to Russia, managed to track this woman down, and married her.

"Al, I'm sorry that I did what I did," Ken said apologetically, referring to his having passed the buck, back when Al had first come to him in search of help. "You came to me for help, and I failed you. But take it from me, I understand it all now . . ."

Al told him that no apology was necessary. Ken then introduced Al and Diane to his wife.

"I have seen you before. You have a birthmark on your back," Ken's wife began without preamble. She was correct. Al does have a birthmark on his back. She turned back to her husband. "I have seen him there, up on the ships . . ."

Diane's jaw dropped. *Up on the ships...?* Al shot her an "I'll explain later" look.

The rest of the night passed pleasantly with Al and Diane mingling for polite conversation. At the end of the night, her curiosity piqued, Diane finally took Al aside and demanded an explanation. Figuring that one was long overdue, he started at the beginning, outlining his experiences with the otherworldly visitors. He could see from the expression on her face that she didn't exactly believe him. Finally, Randy walked over and interjected, "Al's a classic abductee." He went on to not only back up all of Al's claims, but also to offer supporting testimony concerning his own encounters with the feared Men in Black.

His contact with the world of ufology turned out to be too much for Randy, and he would go on to tragically take his own life just a short time later. He left a suicide note that read: "I'm not putting up with this shit for the rest of my life. YOU KEEP 'EM." Al feels strongly that the "them" in question are the extraterrestrial visitors. Randy was in his late forties.

A Rift

In 1990, Al moved into a new home out in Lakewood. The visits continued, but he managed to get through life in coping mode, taking it a day at a time. He began dating another contactee after she walked up to him one day and said, "Don't I know you?"

Al nodded. "Uh huh."

"Is it from . . . where I think it is?"

"Uh huh."

As a consequence of his new-found relationship, the abductions now became double abductions. He and his girlfriend were both taken from either his home or from her apartment, when they spent time there together. On other occasions, she would be abducted from her home and then returned afterward to Al's place, necessitating that he drive her home.

Somehow, as bizarre and surreal as life got for the two abductees, they coped. Life went on as normal (for a given value of normal, at least) amidst the sea of High Strangeness.

Fast forward to 1993. Al was part of a wildland burn project, helping to mitigate the potential dangers of forest fires. The crew was out at the Chatfield Reservoir (near Waterton Canyon where our story first began) just to the south of Littleton. Their work involved carefully lighting backfires using drip torches, burning off some of the dead brush before it could become fuel for a larger conflagration.

Suddenly, out of nowhere, what Al calls a dimensional rift opened up in the air, perhaps a quarter-mile off to the left of the crew of firefighters. Three humanoid figures were standing there already, watching the firefighters go about their business. The air seemed to somehow ripple, passing by like a wave, and in its aftermath there were now six more of the figures, deposited there as though they had just stepped through some kind of doorway.

All were dressed identically, in khaki pants and tan shirts. They gave off a strangely corporate vibe, much like a group of executives holding an impromptu meeting out there in the wilderness.

Where the hell did they come from? Al asked himself, though he didn't have to look far to find an answer to that mostly rhetorical question. They had traveled through the rift. No sooner had the thought entered his head than all nine of the visitors turned to look at him. One of them—

the leader, perhaps—favored him with a polite nod. Al's fellow firefighters seemed totally oblivious to their presence.

The mysterious group came up the path, passing closely by Al's position and affording him a closer look at them. He noticed a certain uniformity to the group's composition. It was a mixture of males and females, each of them very tall—at least six feet in height. The females all had blonde hair, whereas all of the males had light brown hair.

Looking back through the annals of ufology, this class of extraterrestrial visitor (known as the Nordics) appear to have been visiting Earth for a long time: The first recorded reports date back to the 1950s wave of contacts. Nordics always seem to be in prime shape, without an ounce of body fat on their tall, rangy frames, and fair-haired, with skin that is either pale or somewhat tanned. According to those contactees who have encountered the Nordics face to face, their agenda seems to be one that has the best interests of both planet Earth and humanity at heart. Although they have mouths (and, therefore, one can reasonably assume, vocal cords) the Nordics prefer to speak telepathically, beaming their thoughts directly into the mind of the contactee. The typical Nordic contact experience seems to be a very positive one, and the human being tends to be the recipient of feelings of being protected, if not loved, by the extraterrestrials.

All seemed to be fairly young, and their facial features looked similar enough that they could quite easily have been mistaken for a family if you had seen them in a restaurant. None of the Nordics spoke to Al, but simply went on their way, walking off into the distance without so much as a word. The dimensional rift had disappeared without a trace.

Get the Hell Out of Here

Tired of not getting the answers he so desperately craved, Al finally decided to go on the offensive. He set out to find the alien visitors, to face them on his own terms. That was when he decided to do something that, depending upon your point of view, was either very, very brave, or very, very foolish.

He went to Dulce, New Mexico.

Stories of Dulce Base, a rumored secret underground facility, are legion—as are claims of people disappearing in the vicinity, lost without a trace. Guided by some instinctual sense of the aliens' location, Al drove there, parked his car at the side of the road, and walked the final part of his journey on foot.

A black Huey helicopter was on the ground next to him, completely devoid of insignia or markings of any kind. Next to it was a landed saucer, silver in color, which he estimated at some thirty feet in diameter. He had no recollection of getting back to his truck, but the message that he was given by the Greys and their black-garbed allies was a very clear one: Get the hell out of here. Now. Or else.

"They were not happy to see me," Al said soberly, going on to describe a gathering of Greys and US military personnel, all of whom were wearing black uniforms and carrying assault rifles. One officer, wearing the epaulets of a colonel, stomped up to Al angrily. Before the officer could say a word, all of Al's cumulative fear and resentment bubbled up to the surface, spewing out in a torrent of rage.

"I'm freaking done with you!" Al yelled, screaming at the top of his voice. He was going berserk, but really didn't care at this point. Heads turned to look at him, human and alien alike, and then—

He woke up in his truck.

Figuring It Out

As 1993 segued into 1994, more interactions with the Nordics would follow, along with a similarly humanoid alien race, the Pleidians. They developed a habit of walking up to Al at seemingly random times and locations.

"You need to understand who we are," they would communicate telepathically. "We are not them. Calm down. You need to listen. You do understand that there's no threat here? You're safe with us. Please listen."

Based on his interactions with them, Al has become convinced that the Nordics and Pleidians (so-called because they come from the region of the Pleides star cluster) are waging some kind of war with the Greys. That tracks with the testimony of other contactees, who report that the Nordics have often warned them about the malevolent and sinister intentions of the Greys.

Whenever he encountered them, the Pleidians always dressed immaculately ("they looked like they came right out of the pages of *GQ* magazine," he told me with a smile) and always bore the same message of hope and trust. This tracks with the manner in which others have described them, as being almost perfectly beautiful human beings with slightly pointed ears.

One particularly fascinating characteristic of the Pleidian pairs was that whenever Al encountered them (usually in a grocery store) they always stood back to back, "covering one another's six" in fighter pilot parlance. Al explains that this is because the planet Earth is a battle zone for them, and the threat of conflict with another group of aliens is ever-present. When walking, the female Pleidian will always be a step behind the male, and always positioned off to his right.

Al spent a great deal of time interacting with the Pleidians during 1994, soaking up everything like a sponge that they told him about the state of global affairs. It is from them that he learned about the Earth being essentially caught in a crossfire, besieged on all sides by factions that wished it both good and ill.

Deciding to once more take the bull by the horns, Al visited with a psychic who he trusted implicitly, and with her help, he was able to call forward some of the alien groups that had been interacting with and abducting him. He wanted answers, and felt that this was the way to get them. With the psychic's help, Al was able to draw out some of the visitors and get them to communicate with him. She placed him into a trance state via hypnosis.

For the first time ever, he was opening that door on purpose. His stated intent: Figure out what the hell they wanted with him. Why was he at the center of all this?

"They told me that I have chosen to come here," Al related, tears filling his eyes. "I have chosen to be a benefit to humanity. They were telling me that I needed to continue my emergency medical work, because there would be a great need for it during this transition."

"Transition?" I asked curiously. "Transition *to* what? Transition *from* what?"

"They didn't say exactly what, but they implied that it was some kind of big planetary transformation of consciousness. I can tell you that it began in 2012, and it's picking up speed."

I found this statement fascinating because other contactees who I had interviewed for this book had made very similar statements about the Earth currently undergoing a planet-wide upsurge of enlightenment and increased spirituality.

Al had much to think about after those sessions. Sitting in his living room one evening, he was turning the events of a session over and over in his mind, when suddenly he felt both of his hands being violently grabbed. His mouth was pried open by some unseen force. He couldn't open his eyes, which were screwed tightly shut, and he was unable to scream for help.

He is convinced that this was the energy form of a reptilian, trying to force its way inside his body. Al picked up on its thoughts and sensed a great deal of hostility and resentment toward him: The reptilian felt that this was its planet, not his, and what business did he have being here?

Fortunately for Al, the creature wasn't quite strong enough to overcome him. As soon as it had retreated, he called the psychic who had helped him communicate with the alien entities earlier that day. "Jesus Christ!" she exclaimed, "Did you not close the door?!" Al protested that he had shut down the door into their realm, just as he had been instructed. The reptilian had shown up uninvited.

It appeared that stronger measures were needed. Under her direction (and that of another psychic consultant), Al placed a piece of obsidian at each of the four corners of his property, assured that it would bolster the psychic defenses of his home and help keep out any unwanted interlopers. He dutifully buried the four pieces of stone, forming a neat (and hidden) square around his property, and then finally went to bed, satisfied that he had added an extra "security fence" that should allow him to rest a little more peacefully.

The next morning, when Al opened his eyes, all four pieces of obsidian were sitting on his bedroom window ledge, surrounded with clumps of the very same dirt that he had buried them in.

So much for the security fence.

To make matters more interesting, ever since that night, the grass in those four corners of Al's yard has never grown back.

Does the abduction phenomenon have a genetic component? Does it run in families?

Al certainly believes so, and there is much anecdotal evidence from contactees to support the theory.

Al's mother and much of his maternal family grew up in the area of Devil's Creek and Angel Pass, close to the town of Crested Butte. It was a family rule that under no circumstances whatsoever should any member of the family go up to either of those two locations, no matter what the reason. This went doubly for the kids, who liked to run and play outdoors on the steep hillsides and large boulders.

One day, young Al asked his mother why they were not permitted to go anywhere even remotely close to Devil's Creek or Angel Pass. Taking him by surprise, she grabbed him roughly by the shoulders.

"Because we're not welcome there!" she exclaimed, the naked terror visible in her eyes and plain to hear in the shaking of her voice. This was a very common reaction among members of his family, and he cannot help but wonder whether the source of that fear is the same visitors who have plagued him throughout his entire life.

It was still 1994 when Al took his two-year-old nephew on an outing to the Denver Zoo, followed by a trip to the Train Museum. "Uncle Al, come sit with me. I have to talk with you." The way that this statement was delivered—so forthright, matter-of-fact, and plain-old adult-like—made Al do a double-take. This wasn't how two-year-olds usually talked. Al obeyed, taking a seat on a bench next to the young boy.

"I've got to ask you something, and you have to tell me the truth." The tone and timbre of the boy's speech were totally serious, and seemed to assume a turn of phrase that would be more at home in the mouth of a twenty-two-year-old. "Do the little blue doctors come and visit you?"

Without intending to, Al immediately burst into tears. Here was his worst fear, validated and made flesh: His young nephew was now subject to the same abduction experiences that he himself was.

"Mom says to pray to God that they go away, but they don't."

Al was becoming visibly upset as he recounted this incident to me. I offered him a break, but he refused with a fervent shake of the head. He was coming to the end of his story, and it was almost as if he was relying on momentum to get through it, to help him overcome the burned-in message that this was something that he wasn't supposed to talk about with anybody— let alone an author who was going to recount his story to the world.

He went on to explain that what his nephew referred to as the "little blue doctors" were the classic Greys made famous by Whitley Strieber in his book *Communion*. The boy was being abducted and returned by them on a regular basis, at the age of two . . . and frankly, who knew how much younger?

Al himself claims to be regularly taken to this very day. He has found a way to live with being an abductee, to come to terms with it as best he possibly can, and yet the experience is still a traumatic one and seems to have left him with many emotional scars. He still struggles to make sense of it all, having been told conflicting stories by some of the extraterrestrial (and, of course, human) beings he has come into contact with.

The Grand Theme

I asked Al about the grand scheme that arches above the entire extraterrestrial abduction phenomenon.

"The Earth is an experiment," he began, speaking slowly and searching for the best way to put it. "This planet primarily belongs to the lizard race. Let's go back 12,500 years. Atlantis still existed. Lemuria still existed, and it belonged to the lizards." (Lemuria is the name given to a land at the center of an enduring "lost continent" myth, which is said to have sunk beneath the ocean in the aftermath of some global catastrophe.) "The Greys and the Praying Mantises had possession of Atlantis.

"Now, you—your energy, soul, spirit essence, call it whatever you want—make a choice to come here and incarnate. You manifest as whichever species you want . . . human, Grey, lizard, mantis, whatever. Once you arrive in your physical form, you're there until you are allowed to leave . . . and that can be a long time. You have to learn the ropes of your chosen species. Learn to be a human, learn to eat with a fork and not go to the toilet in the street—all the things that make us, us."

Al goes on to state that according to three different psychic mediums, he has been told that his soul incarnated here 12,500 years ago, and that he came with one singular purpose in mind: to help others. His soul was "very young, immature, and stupid."

He claims that the Greys live on human fear, feeding upon our negative emotions for their sustenance. The more frightened a human being becomes, the happier they are.

The Praying Mantises are aloof and indifferent, seemingly unconcerned with the way in which human beings feel or react.

Al's description of these races is very consistent with that of other abductees and contactees, not to mention the vast array of ufology literature. The Greys tend to be somewhere in the vicinity of three to four feet in height, and are rarely more than fifty pounds in weight.

The extraterrestrials responsible for abducting Betty and Barney Hill in New Hampshire in 1961—arguably the first "mainstream" abduction case, particularly as it was soon made into a TV movie starring James Earl Jones—look a lot like the Greys, if one looks at the Hills' sketches. We take the abduction scenario for granted today, but it is important to remember that practically nobody had heard of such things back in the early sixties. Sure, the contactee phenomenon was in full swing, but the aliens who were making themselves known to the contactees were almost always human-like (if not completely human) in appearance, extraordinarily handsome or beautiful, and above all else, friendly.

The creatures who abducted the Hills, on the other hand, took them without their permission, scooping them up into their craft in the middle of a dark and lonely stretch of road; they then experimented on the Hills, driving a sharp needle directly into Betty's navel. The entire case is documented in John Fuller's fascinating book *The Interrupted Journey*. It was not long after the book and TV movie came out that the "little grey men" trope first entered the public consciousness.

It has never left.

So what *are* the Greys? Common consensus holds that they are a sort of "galactic parasite," preying upon the humanoid species of the galaxy for their own advantage. Many sources maintain that the Greys have been known to the United States government since at least the 1950s, when President Dwight D. Eisenhower's administration is rumored by whistleblowers to have cut a clandestine deal with them: tacit permission to abduct and experiment upon human beings, in exchange for sharing some of their technology. On a more worrying note, those same whistleblowers report that this "deal with the devil" was made primarily because the American government knew full well that it lacked the capability of protecting its citizens if the Greys decided to go ahead and take what they wanted anyway.

Although I am putting this in rather simplistic terms, the emerging story of extraterrestrial contact has both its good guys and its bad guys . . . and the Greys are most definitely among the latter. In fact, it is difficult to identify any worse offenders. They seem to take whoever and whatever they want, and spare no thought for the consequences.

If the whistleblowers now stepping forward are to be believed, the Greys are engaged in a worldwide mass abduction project whose victims number in the millions.

Author and channeler Barry Strohm claims to have made contact with the spirit of an advanced extraterrestrial entity named Mou. Mou was only too willing to answer Barry's questions, and the fascinating results of this paranormal Q&A were published in Barry's book *Aliens Among Us*.

Needless to say, Barry wanted to get to the bottom of the abduction phenomenon, and asked Mou to shed some light on the enigma.

Mou responded with the rather disconcerting statement that if the Greys were not ruled by The Council (a governing body composed of beings from various planets) then they would have taken over the Earth by now!

When trying to put it all into context, Al describes the Earth as "an experiment gone awry." Earth is a sort of intergalactic crossroads, among other things, and has become the focal point of many different extraterrestrial races, each of which has their own different agenda. Some of those agendas will benefit humanity, whereas others most assuredly will not.

Only time will tell which of them will ultimately prevail.

As for Al, he continues to lead a meaningful and productive life, and still deals with the extraterrestrial contact phenomenon on a regular basis—which only goes to show that, of all the many species that are said to populate our galaxy, humankind may well be the most resilient . . .

CHAPTER 5.

MUTILATED

For many years now, something extremely strange has been happening in the region of southern Colorado, close to the border of New Mexico, known as the San Luis Valley—something very, very disturbing indeed.

Not that this is anything particularly new. The area has long been known as a UFO hotspot, with stories dating back to the mid-1960s, when the area acquired a reputation for mysterious lights in the sky . . . and the equally mysterious butchery and bizarre dissection of livestock. It was during this time that the subject of cattle mutilation first entered the public consciousness, with reports coming in from all around the United States by the end of the decade . . .

. . . but one of the very first reports involved a poor horse from Alamosa named Snippy.

Despite the mass of rumors and legends that have swirled up around the case, the name of the mare in question wasn't Snippy at all: her *actual* name was Lady. Yet so badly had the poor creature been carved up by forces unknown, that her corpse was given that distinctly unappetizing nickname by members of the press, when they reported on the incident some weeks afterward.

It was September 8, 1967, when rancher Harry King found the unfortunate creature's dead body lying on a desolate, out-of-the-way stretch of ground on his property not far from the town of Alamosa. Harry, his brother Ben, plus their sister Nellie and her husband Berle, all lived on the ranch, along with the Kings' mother Agnes.

Lady had been missing since the day before. When interviewed, Harry would say that he had suspected the worst when the three-year-old mare did not join the other horses for their usual feed.

At first, Harry thought that a natural predator had attacked and killed the horse, for the flesh had been stripped from its neck, but the more closely he looked at the body, the less that particular explanation seemed to fit. The skin and underlying tissue hadn't been ripped and torn away raggedly, as jaws and claws were wont to do, but rather had been sliced away with near-surgical precision.

Sliced.

Cut.

Snipped.

Besides, King thought to himself as he squatted down to take in the scene, where were the animal tracks leading away from the carcass? The area surrounding Snippy's body bore no such telltale signs of it being dragged there and abandoned, not to mention the fact that the majority of the meat on those bleached-white bones hadn't been touched. Neither was there a blood trail—not even a single scarlet drop anywhere to be seen in proximity to the dead creature. Whatever method had been used to kill Snippy had been remarkably bloodless, and it would subsequently be said that not a drop of blood remained inside the animal's body.

When it was later opened during an impromptu autopsy, Snippy's cranial vault was found to be completely empty. Normally after death, even in hot conditions such as those found commonly in the San Luis, a veterinarian would expect to find traces or brain matter, however small, or at the very least, traces of water. Snippy's brain pan was completely dry.

Her eyes had also been removed. The heart and lungs had been cut out and taken to who knew where. Despite the skin having been partially removed, Snippy's skeleton remained anatomically intact.

Nellie Lewis wasted no time in pointing a finger at who she believed was the guilty party: aliens.

A series of circular marks—the October 1967 *Associated Press* account claims that they were exhaust burns—on a one hundred-foot by fifty-foot stretch of ground nearby only fueled the impression that a flying saucer had landed in the vicinity. When Harry King searched the area a little more thoroughly, he claimed to have found six indentations in the ground that formed a circle some three feet in diameter.

Unwisely picking up a piece of Snippy's flesh, Nellie found it to be extremely sticky to the touch. Within seconds, it was burning the skin of her hand, forcing her to drop it. The part of her hand that had been in contact with the dead horse tissue had turned bright red and continued to ache painfully until Nellie rinsed her hands in water. A 2006 *Denver Post* article by Rich Tosches quotes eyewitness Sylvia Lobato (whose mother was the best friend of Nellie Lewis) as saying: "From the neck up, that horse was peeled. It was just pure white bones. The horse had only been dead for a night, but it looked like it had been dead for months. Nellie was there with us, and she found a piece of metal next to the horse. It was covered in horse hair. When she picked it up, it burned her hand, and she screamed and dropped it. Her hand was badly burned. I was there. I saw it."

Fearing the presence of an extraterrestrial power, she pleaded with the authorities to look into the case. Local law enforcement was dismissive, with the local sheriff writing the bizarre episode off as nothing more than a lightning strike—a simple case of the poor horse being in the wrong place at the wrong time. This prognosis was made from the comfort of Sheriff Ben Philips' office chair, and made for pretty weak sauce. When those who had actually set eyes upon the beast's corpse pointed out that lightning strikes tend to leave entrance (and sometimes exit) burns in a distinctive leaf pattern known to medical professionals as "ferning," Sheriff Philips had no credible answer.

Fortunately, representatives of the US Forest Service were a little more inquisitive, listening patiently to her account and then dispatching a ranger to investigate further. Carrying a Geiger counter out to the scene of what was beginning to look like a crime, the ranger was surprised to discover that the background radiation was high in the area, especially in the vicinity of the indentations in the earth, but then trailed off towards normal as he approached the carcass itself.

Clearly, *something* was afoot . . . but what? Nellie's conviction that forces from another world were at work was further buttressed by an unusually high number of UFO sightings in the local area, including one that had flown over the ranch on the day that Snippy had last been seen, according to Harry King's elderly mother, Agnes.

As time passed, the tale grew even stranger in the telling. Several scientists and pathologists were drafted in to perform post-mortem tests on the carcass, each with differing results.

Meanwhile, at the University of Colorado in Boulder, the Condon Committee (known also as "the Colorado Project" and "the Colorado Study") was firing on all cylinders. Running from 1966 to 1968, this intensive academic study of aerial phenomena was funded by the United States Air Force, and its stated intent was to address the wave of UFO-related mass hysteria that was sweeping the nation. The final Condon Report findings essentially concluded that there was nothing to the mass of UFO sightings reported from coast to coast, attributing them to such natural (and blatantly ridiculous) findings as swamp gas, hallucinations, and planets such as Venus and Jupiter.

Dr. Fred Ayers (a pathologist) and Dr. Robert Adams—associated with the School of Veterinary Medicine at Colorado State University—were brought in to examine Snippy's remains, with an eye to assessing the claims of extraterrestrial intervention. Their findings were damning so far as the alien angle was concerned. The two veterinary professionals saw nothing unusual with Lady's corpse.

The horse's leg had been badly infected, Adams reported, and the unfortunate animal would probably have been suffering badly . . . so badly, in fact, that her throat had been cut, probably in order to spare her from any further pain. Local wildlife had almost certainly denuded the rest of poor Snippy's missing flesh, he claimed, which also explained why the abdominal and thoracic organs were missing, too. The gist seemed to be that coyotes bore far more blame for the state of the carcass than the ubiquitous "little green men" did.

But what of the brain? Liquefied, and then evaporated, Adams concluded neatly.

No aliens required.

Never mind the fact that the wound edges were razor sharp and precise, the cuts far cleaner than anything that hunting knives and other portable skinning tools could achieve.

"I know it's going to pop the bubble," Adams said, acknowledging the now-global fascination with the case, "but the horse was not killed by a flying saucer."

Dr. John H. Altshuler, a Denver-based expert in hematology, and both clinical and anatomic pathology, saw things somewhat differently. Years after examining Snippy's body, he maintained that the black-edged cuts (which almost appeared to be cauterized) were performed in so neat and precise a manner that it was ". . . almost as if they had been cauterized by a modern-day laser. But there was no cauterizing laser technology like that in 1967."

Altshuler hypothesized that Snippy's internal organs had not been removed physically by predators, but rather had been subjected to a heat so intense that it had also cooked the small amount of hemoglobin that remained inside the body. According to Dr. Altshuler, there was no known technology on Earth at the time that could have accounted for the manner of Snippy's dissection—most certainly not the gnawing of hungry predators and carrion birds.

Once all of the remaining flesh and tissue had been boiled away from the bones by a local vet who had acquired Snippy's remains, he was nonplussed to find two holes in the bones of the creature's thigh and pelvis that looked suspiciously like bullet entrance wounds. To him, the mystery of Snippy's death was now solved: Local kids or sick thrill-seekers had used the horse for target practice, putting a pair of rounds into her and spooking her so badly that, panicked and half-crazed with pain, she ran headlong into a barbed-wire fence, thereby accounting for the incision in her throat.

Just how the incision made by a barbed-wire fence happened to be perfectly linear and with a cauterized edge, is something that his explanation is clearly lacking.

For her part, Nellie Lewis stuck to her guns and flatly refused to believe any theory other than the extraterrestrial one, and until her dying day told anybody who would listen that the government was lying about the facts of the Snippy mutilation case, and all about the UFO sightings that she (and a number of her friends) had made in the vicinity of their ranch . . . sightings that continue to the present day.

So whatever happened to poor old Snippy's skeleton? It was mounted for display in a manner similar to that of skeletons that one might find in a museum, and disappeared for a few years before it came into the possession of a private owner, who put it up for auction on eBay in 2006–2008.

The asking price was an overly optimistic $30,000. The highest bid didn't even come close, and so the bleached white bones of the world's best-known mutilated animals stayed with their owner. To the best of my knowledge, they remain there at the time of writing.

Christopher O'Brien Interview

One of the foremost authorities on the Snippy mutilation case (and indeed, on the entire San Luis Valley as a whole) is researcher Christopher O'Brien, who spent thirteen years living in and investigating accounts of bizarre activity in the San Luis Valley, writing three books in the process.

I interviewed Christopher following the publication of his most recent book, the excellent *Stalking the Herd: Unraveling the Cattle Mutilation Mystery,* a well-researched and superbly written work that I encourage anybody who wishes to gain a broader understanding of the cattle mutilation enigma to seek out.

Christopher has personally interviewed a number of the key players in the Snippy case, including Berle Lewis, Nellie's husband. He combed through a huge stack of newspaper articles and other supporting documentation, cross-checking and referencing the facts reported therein. His conclusion: When it comes to the Snippy case, researchers find themselves in murky waters indeed, for the tale has grown in the telling, and many of the supposed "facts" listed in those articles are contradictory, confusing, and often just plain wrong.

O'Brien points out that before the Snippy case hit the mainstream media, the concept of animal mutilation was something unknown to the average person in the street. Perhaps more importantly, he describes this particular mutilation as the "ground zero" case for establishing the link between animal mutilation and the UFO phenomenon. The UFO aspect was a large part of what dragged poor Snippy into the public eye in the first place: After all, the many tabloid headlines that screamed "ALIENS KILLED MY HORSE!" sold *a lot* of newspapers. Prior to October 1967, when variations on this article thrilled and fascinated newspaper readers around the world, it seemed that nobody had considered a possible connection between extraterrestrials and bizarrely-slaughtered animals.

Ever since then, "cattle mutilation" equals "aliens"—in the public consciousness, at least. It is a meme that has worked its way into every aspect of popular culture, and shows no signs of abating any time soon. And yet, in a revelation that genuinely took me aback, Christopher told me that he personally believes UFOs and their occupants to be one of the less likely culprits. At the very least, the so-called "extraterrestrial hypothesis" is just one in a series of possible explanations.

In Christopher's view, clandestine governmental programs, not to mention those run by private entities such as corporations, are every bit as likely to be responsible for the widespread illegal capture, dissection, and dumping of these animal carcasses. Nor can the possibility of secret military experiments and weapons tests be discounted. When I mentioned my background as a paranormal investigator, our conversation quickly turned toward the subject of the many similarities that the fields of ufology and paranormal investigation share.

"We may be dealing with the same phenomenon," Christopher concluded, "but coming at it from different angles."

It is an intriguing possibility. One thing that we can say for sure, however, is that the animal mutilation phenomenon in Colorado, has followed us into the twenty-first century. In a 2009 *Denver Post* article ("*Colorado Cow Mutilations Baffle Ranchers, Cops, UFO Believer*") reporter Jason Blevins details a case in which four calves were somehow butchered overnight. Their guts were gone, along with their tongues; in a scene that will now be all too familiar, sections of flesh were removed with almost surgical precision, the incisions running in perfectly straight lines as they slice through the animal hide and underlying tissue.

Yet again, the killings left behind not a single drop of blood, and no tracks were found in the vicinity that might lend a conventional explanation. However the animals were killed and mutilated, it either had to be done somewhere else, with the creatures being drained of blood, after which they were unceremoniously deposited in the wilderness to be found once more, or some as-yet-unidentified technology is at work, one that is capable of somehow slaughtering and then partially dissecting the cows without leaving any trace of struggle or hemorrhage behind.

And the location of this mysterious act of butchery? Why, the San Luis Valley, of course.

Such cases of bizarre cattle death and mutilation occur on an annual basis throughout the state of Colorado, but it is fair to say that the San Luis Valley sees more than its fair share of them.

Just as it does with UFOs . . .

CHAPTER 6.
ALL ALONG THE WATCHTOWER

Judy Messoline had not the slightest intention of getting into the UFO business when she relocated to a plot of land in the San Luis Valley in the mid-1990s, a couple of miles north of the town of Hooper. Her mind was firmly set on the idea of raising and selling cattle. The cattle business turned out not to be a raging success. With a laugh, Judy told me that, "Cattle don't want to eat sand!"

Nevertheless, she tried her best to make it a going concern for five years. When it finally became evident that the cattle venture was going to be a dead end, Plan B came right out of left field: build a UFO watchtower!

It was impossible to live in the San Luis Valley for any appreciable length of time without encountering the strange lights in the sky for which the region is renowned. In part, this can be attributed to the geography of the region: Its wide, sparse vistas are mostly devoid of human habitation, and at an altitude of more than 7,500 feet—just short of a mile-and-a-half above sea level, along with crystal clear skies—it is the perfect place to experience the UFO phenomenon first hand. Perhaps most importantly of all, there was almost nothing in the way of light pollution to spoil the show above your head.

On more than one occasion, Judy has encountered trespassers on her land, many of whom sheepishly admitted that they were out there with the intent of photographing UFOs. With a friendly shrug and a smile, she'd offer a pleasant word and simply leave them to it; but the idea of catering to the UFO enthusiasts wouldn't go away, and she finally decided "what the hell" and just ran with it. Selling off the remainder of her cattle herd in order to finance her new dream, she enlisted some help in the form of friends with construction skills, and got right down to work.

Construction started on Judy's pet project in late 1999, and would finally be completed by the middle of 2000, just in time for the summer season. A campsite came first; Judy envisioned it as simply a place for visitors to pitch their tents, kick back in a lawn chair, and take in the activity in the skies above. Next came a small dome, which functioned as a gift shop selling alien-themed mementoes and souvenirs, along with a few necessities such as snacks.

Lastly came the *piece de resistance*, a ten-foot-high scaffold platform that would serve as an observation platform, the UFO Watchtower, after which the entire site would soon be named. Judy had fairly modest expectations at first, figuring that a handful of people at most would visit this isolated location each year, mostly during the summer when the weather was at its best. She had no idea of the extent to which her pride and joy would take off: At the time of writing (the summer of 2016) more than 30,000 visitors have come to the Watchtower, an average of just under 2,000 people each year.

The first visitors were mostly curious locals, interested to see what was going on with the metal platform and stucco dome out in the middle of nowhere. Then the UFO community got word. They flocked to the Watchtower in droves, bringing bucket-loads of cameras and scientific equipment along with them.

Before she knew it, Judy had become a sort of "central clearing house" for every UFO sighting and alien encounter within her part of the valley. She began to write them all down in log books, chronicling not only the sightings that visitors to her tower told her about, but also those that span the rest of the San Luis Valley. Her archive has expanded tenfold since she recorded her very first UFO story and shows no sign of slowing down any time soon.

Many who claim to be psychic mediums have visited the Watchtower over the years, and all have told a similar story: It has been built on grounds where two invisible energy vortexes can be found. I asked her if she had known this at the time. "Not at all," she chuckled, "at least, not consciously. But I'm pretty sure that I sensed those energies. It's almost as if I was guided to this place."

Every bit as intriguing as the vortexes are those who Judy claims are their guardians: two energy-form entities who serve as invisible gatekeepers and protectors. It has become traditional for visitors to the UFO Watchtower to leave a small token in the area as an offering; in return, they are permitted to make one request of the energies there. Some ask for healing, others for guidance. The variety of requests spans the entire spectrum. Judy maintains that many of those requests are nonetheless granted, and usually in a very timely manner.

"I don't know if they're angels, aliens, or some other kind of entity," Judy admits, "but I know that they're real. Twenty-five different psychics have all independently told me so."

The array of assorted bric-a-brac has gotten pretty large over the years, so much so that Judy refers to it as her "healing garden."

Ever since that opening in the summer of 2000, the UFO sightings have continued unabated. Most sightings take place during the summer months, primarily because that's when there are always observers at the tower. Although the UFO activity could be every bit as persistent during the colder winter months, there is nobody there to witness and record it—which means that the hundreds of bizarre aerial phenomena reported from the tower may actually be under-reported.

As the Watchtower's proprietor and long-term custodian, it should come as no surprise that Judy has seen more than her fair share of them herself. She recalls seeing what at first seemed to be a satellite, moving sedately across the sky at high altitude on a perfectly straight course one night. The object suddenly stopped dead, hesitated for a moment, and shot straight up in the air, finally disappearing from sight.

When pressed on the subject of her most fascinating experience at the Watchtower, Judy talks of a sighting that took place on May 30, 2016, just a few days prior to our interview. The spherical yellow object was originally mistaken for the Moon, until observers realized that it was outlined in a red glow.

It is intriguing to note that a UFO matching its description almost identically was reported in September 2015, near the town of Antonito, and again one month later near Crestone. The same UFO was seen in different parts of the valley, by multiple observers, and on three separate occasions. Whatever it is, it certainly gets around.

Judy is convinced that whatever people say of the UFOs that flock to the Watchtower, the vast majority of them are extraterrestrial, rather than products of secret governmental research. They have been seen to conduct maneuvers that would be physically impossible for a human pilot to describe; pulling that many Gs (gravities) would smear our feeble bodies all over the interior of the craft, unless some sort of highly sophisticated inertial dampening system was deployed. Human technology certainly has nothing of the sort on the drawing board right now, or for the foreseeable future.

Whenever serving members of the United States Air Force pay the Watchtower a visit, Judy makes a point to ask them about the possibility of the UFOs being something that is fielded by the USAF. The answer is always the same: Nothing in the US military's aerial arsenal can sustain that kind of maneuvering. The sheer speed at which the UFOs can stop in mid-air, pivot, and turn on a dime is said to be nothing short of breathtaking.

"You can never count on when you're going to see something," Judy laughed. "The most active time seems to be between eleven o'clock at night and three in the morning—though we do get plenty of daytime sightings too."

That struck a chord with me. In my twenty years as a paranormal investigator, I have often remarked upon the fact that the most active hours tend to be between eleven and three, before things usually peter out with the onset of the dawn: Yet another link between the world of the ghostly and that of the UFO.

The UFO Watchtower has also seen its share of visitors who were every bit as fascinating as the location itself. Serving members of the Air Force are frequent visitors, hardly surprising when one considers the proximity of the USAF Academy in Colorado Springs, Cheyenne Mountain, and other similar military installations. UFO hunters from all around the world make it a port of call when seeking to capture evidence of those elusive lights in the sky, as do day-trippers and road-trippers alike.

But what of the extraterrestrials themselves—surely, with the entire San Luis Valley being such a massive UFO sighting hotspot, the occupants of some of those craft must be tempted to slip away every once in a while and check out the Watchtower for themselves?

"One or two," Judy chuckles, when I asked her about visitors dropping by who claim to come from beyond this world. She goes on to describe a variety of men and women who look, sound, and act like those described by the contactees whose accounts are related elsewhere in this book. Her words bring to mind images of the Nordics, the Pleidians, and the other humanoid races that many in the UFO community believe are walking among us without our knowledge.

Is it possible that extraterrestrial visitors really are dropping by the UFO Watchtower, and if so, why? "To keep an eye on things," Judy replies, as if that explains everything. And perhaps it does. What better place to keep a finger on the pulse of humanity's ever-evolving attitude toward the subject of UFOs, after all, than this quirky oasis in the mystical San Luis Valley?

I asked Judy about her plans for the future, so far as the Watchtower was concerned. Was some kind of further expansion in order, developing the site to do more things, perhaps? Refreshingly, in a day and age in which everybody seems to be pushing towards that next big thing, Judy is resolutely prepared to keep on doing what she is doing: watching the skies around Hooper and the San Luis Valley and keeping track of the many visitors who like to drop in . . . whether they come from this world, or far beyond it.

CHAPTER 7.
GALACTIC CITIZENSHIP

One of the most common accusations leveled against eyewitnesses who report a UFO sighting is that they don't know what they are looking at. In a sense, that is somewhat understandable: After all, objects as diverse as airplanes, helicopters, balloons, lightning, meteorites, natural atmospheric phenomena, and brightly shining planets, such as Venus and Jupiter, are often mistaken for UFOs.

But what of witnesses who are highly trained observers, skilled and experienced in identifying airborne objects?

One such man is Don Daniels. For as long as he can remember, Don has been fascinated with the sky and all things that fly; this is doubtless why he pursued a career in aviation, becoming firstly a flight instructor and charter pilot, then when the airlines were not hiring due to de-regulation, he became an air traffic controller for eight years, and eventually became an airline pilot. Over his decades as an aviator (Don took his first formal flying lessons at the age of fourteen so he could be a qualified copilot with his dad on family trips and soloed on his sixteenth birthday, the youngest you can solo a powered plane) he has seen pretty much everything that flies, whether natural or artificial in origin. He is not a man that is easily fooled . . .

. . . which only serves to make his story all the more remarkable.

Alongside his love for aviation, Don has always been an extremely passionate fan of science fiction. As a boy, he spent hours engrossed in the worlds of Robert A. Heinlein, Arthur C. Clarke, Isaac Asimov, and a host of other writers who explored the frontiers of science and the potential of extraterrestrial life. He was also an avid fan of *Star Trek*, (especially the *Next Generation* series) finding that its message of universal peace, compassion, and curiosity resonated deeply within him; on the big screen, *Flight of the Navigator, Close Encounters of the Third Kind*, the original *The Day the Earth Stood Still*, and other Hollywood movies that showed audiences benevolent alien visitors only made him more enthusiastic about the subject of all things extraterrestrial.

Expressing a belief in the UFO phenomenon has always been something akin to the kiss of death for an airline pilot's career, and so Don played his cards very close to his chest where his personal beliefs were concerned, not wanting to be tagged as a believer in "little green men." Nonetheless, he continued to keep an enquiring mind, attending conferences and seminars on the subject during his spare time, and reading everything that he possibly could.

Don's first true UFO sighting took place in 1999. He was on an expedition one moonless night to the Baca, near Crestone in the San Luis Valley, with a group from the Center for the Study of Extra-Terrestrial Intelligence (CSETI). Don was careful to keep not only his eyes but also his mind as open as possible, without being gullible in the process. All was peaceful and quiet. Then, what seemed to be something that looked not quite like a meteorite streaked down towards the horizon from high above their heads, with a vaporous plasma tail playing out behind it.

As the CSETI observers watched with bated breath, the "meteorite" suddenly came to an abrupt instant stop, seeming to hover in the sky just about twenty degrees above the distant southwest horizon. It grew steadily brighter, until it was more luminous than any of the stars and planets scattered around the sky that evening. It was a big blue/white light, bigger and brighter than even Venus. Without reference or seeing any physical structure, it is impossible to judge distance on a light in the night sky, but they got the impression that it was between two and twenty miles away.

Don knew immediately that whatever this thing was, it was no shooting star.

Dr. Steven Greer, the international director of CSETI, seemed completely unfazed by this strange turn of events, as though he had seen something very much like it before. Reaching into his pocket for a laser pointer, Dr. Greer flashed it twice in the direction of the as-yet-unidentified object.

The UFO pulsed twice in return.

Others in the group used a spotlight to flash at the UFO. Once again, it responded in kind. Don was seriously impressed. No known Earth-based craft could have made such a sudden stop: Its inhabitants would have been turned to mush by the sheer number of Gs that were pulled. The only reasonable explanation was either an extra-dimensional or extra-terrestrial one.

Whoever (or whatever) it was, Don and his companions had just initiated contact . . . and gotten a response. Communication was taking place.

Don was about to suggest that they try using a prime number sequence, and see if they could alternate numbers, when the object emitted a beam of pale blue/white light, bathing the assembled CSETI observers in a circle of light. Then some members of the group, including Don, observed a redundant line in the beam sweep through them all, performing a scan of some sort, and then retracted slowly back into the craft once more, getting shorter instead of just switching off, as if it was made of something more tangible and substantial than mere photons.

When I sat down with Don for the first of several interviews, he was very frank about the fact that his entire worldview changed at that moment: "I knew—not just believed, but absolutely knew—that the UFO phenomenon was real, and that I had just made contact with it. That changed everything."

Don would return to the region of the Great Sand Dunes many times, searching for answers and further contact with the unexplained. On more than one occasion, he would find it. Alien craft put on spectacular performances, much as military pilots do for crowds of spectators at an air show. The craft seemed to defy the laws of physics as we currently understand them, dropping suddenly and curving in from high altitude at death-defying speeds, only to "phase out" before slamming into the desert floor. While it is conceivable that Don could have witnessed unmanned drones, the current level of acknowledged human aviation technology is far beneath that required to explain the performances that he saw.

A few days later, Don began to perceive patterns of unusual lights, which finally coalesced into what seemed to be the shape of a humanoid form. At first questioning his own mental faculties, he was relieved to find that others in the CSETI group were able to see them, too. A little energy work performed by skilled practitioners strengthened his ability to see the forms more clearly the next night, allowing him to make them out in greater detail: five feet tall with a pointed chin and a human-like nose and mouth. Their eyes were subtly different, larger and shaped like almonds. The head was supported by a very thin neck, and the entire build of the creatures was lithe and athletic. It must be emphasized that these were not remotely the classic Greys made popular by Whitley Strieber's *Communion*.

Most importantly of all, there was absolutely no sense of fear. Don is very much an advocate of the human-alien contact experience being one of joy and wonder for the most part (particularly if one is in the correct frame of mind) and certainly not the horrific nightmare that some Hollywood movies would have us believe. Attempting to communicate with the closest of these visitors, Don sent what he hoped was a telepathic message identifying himself and his good intentions.

The response was also non-verbal: an almost overwhelming sense of love, universal and unconditional, followed by a feeling of sheer gratitude. In his written account of the incident (the intriguing *Evolution Through Contact: Becoming a Galactic Cosmic Citizen*) Don describes it thusly:

- Confused a bit by the telepathic impression of Intense Gratitude, the moment I mentally said "Huh?" the impression came back that they were grateful that there was anyone on this dysfunctional planet who wanted peaceful relations with them, when what they generally encountered was the covert military guys trying to shoot them down.

It is important to mention that while Don's contact experience has been primarily a positive and enlightening one, that has not been entirely the case. A couple of years after his first encounter with the light form entity, he and fellow CSETI members experienced something akin to a psychic attack: a feeling of overwhelming evil and coldness, which Don attributes not to extraterrestrial influence, but rather to that of specially-trained covert government operatives who were under orders to derail the good work that was being carried out. He describes it as "a psychotronic attack or abduction attempt," and likes to point out that it can be counteracted by going deep within oneself in meditation, heading to a point where one is beyond ego, at one with the universe, and beyond fear. In this way, Don says, the attackers have nothing to latch onto, as they work using your own fears as a purchase point, and will try to hook the ego or sense of separateness we all have. He is convinced that divorcing oneself from the ego and instead working to transcend such petty human concerns and becoming one with higher, nobler ideals, is the way to oppose such negative interactions.

Don continued to study, ask questions, and attend conferences and retreats, working to develop his remote viewing abilities. During the course of a guided meditation, Don's worldview expanded exponentially once again, when he learned something of the grand scheme of things out there in the reaches of space. Dr. Greer talks about an organization known as the Interplanetary Council, which oversees the multitude of myriad races that inhabit our galaxy, where the older (and presumably wiser) civilizations watch over those that are less mature—such as our own. In meditation, the entire group was led to the Council chambers for a visit, and Don established a connection that would last with one of the Council members.

During this period of experiences, Don happened to be flying and enjoying a layover in San Antonio, Texas. He was still assimilating the incredible events surrounding his time with CSETI, and learning to look at the universe in an entirely different way. Off-duty and between flights, he and another pilot found their way into a bar that was hosting an open mic night.

The two aviators sat and enjoyed the constant stream of stand-up performances, ranging from comedy to music to poetry, where the amateurism was more than offset by the enthusiasm of the performers. One poem, titled *Star Child*, struck a nerve and really activated something within Don; as he sat there listening to verse after verse, the pilot began to receive what he describes as "an intuitive flow, or download." He found that he simply couldn't get it out of his head. Pretty soon Don was reaching out to snatch up napkins from across the table, and began to scribble his own lines of poetry. The words were coming from somewhere deep within him, and refused to stop flowing even when he had left the bar and returned to his hotel room for the night. Nor could he sleep; in that hypnogogic borderline state on the verge of sleep the words continued to wake him, demanding that he write them down on the paper that now sat by his bedside.

The end result was a poem that Don called *Friends in High Places,* which is replete with themes of oneness, unity, and above all, of humanity taking its place in the greater galactic community.

He had taken another step on the road to becoming a cosmic citizen.

Declassified

By the time 2001 came around, Don was to become involved with an attempt to get information about the UFO phenomenon officially declassified and disseminated to the public at large. The Disclosure Project, as it is known, was putting on an event at the National Press Club in Washington, DC.

The list of speakers, headed up by Dr. Greer, incorporated all manner of credible eyewitnesses, the vast majority of them coming from a military, scientific, or academic background. They all had one aim: to prove that the truth really was out there, and to get it out in front of the public.

Over the course of the next five days, Don and his colleagues heard some of the most incredible testimony imaginable, a veritable mountain of information that bore witness to the reality of the UFO phenomenon. Unfortunately—but sadly, very predictably—the mainstream media in the US all but ignored the Disclosure Project, consigning it to the back burner. Few outlets gave it more than a cursory mention or a few scant column inches at best. The news was much better received around the world, and Don reports that media experts estimated that about 2 billion people (about a third of the world's population) saw the story in one form or another.

Here in the United States, the story was buried.

Not long afterward, in what seems like awfully coincidental timing, Don ran into trouble at the airline when a coworker reported him to management due to (of all things) a *Star Trek* Starfleet Command laminated ID card, which he kept in his wallet. The implication was that Don took "all of this UFO stuff" a little too seriously, perhaps to the point where his sanity ought to be called into question. The end result of this was that Don found himself slapped with a mandatory appointment with the company psychiatrist.

Fortunately, the doctor happened to be an eminently reasonable man. He accepted Don's explanations at face value, and presented him with a signed letter stating that he was "certified sane." A dubious distinction for a pilot, but we all should be so lucky . . .

Although he found every aspect of the UFO phenomenon to be fascinating, the area that held the greatest interest for him was that of geopolitics. Don found that it occupied more and more of his thinking. The link between extraterrestrial technology and the associated potential for clean, unlimited energy seemed tantalizingly close, and would change the world forever (for the better, one hoped) if that potential could be realized in the best interest of mankind.

Keeping Up

In addition to forming a small group of Denver-based contactees, with the intention of mutually supporting each other and learning from one another's experiences, Don made a point of keeping up with his friends at CSETI, taking annual field trips with them to areas of high UFO activity. It was on one such trip that Don underwent an incredible encounter. Sitting quietly and conducting an exercise in remote viewing, he went into a meditative state and invited any extraterrestrials who happened to be in the neighborhood to "either drop by and say hello, come on down and play," or failing that, to beam/bring him up to their ship for a visit.

Somebody was evidently listening, because Don was immediately transported aboard an extraterrestrial craft and deposited straight into their main control room. Looking around, he was amazed to find himself surrounded by a bunch of what he describes as "crustacean creatures," none larger than a small child in height. They were communicating with each other and attempted to speak with Don using a language composed almost entirely of throat clicking noises.

Concerned that he must be terribly intimidating to these beings as he was twice as tall as them, he squatted down on the floor to get to their level, trying to make himself less intimidating and more accessible to their tiny frames. The creatures had pincers where a human being would have hands, and in no time at all a couple of them began to gently touch him, giving free expression to their natural curiosity.

"I did not get the impression that they were interested in my anatomy," he says, "but rather that they were already very familiar with us, and were mostly curious about this particular human who gave permission and was willing to put himself out there for contact. Since I could feel them, it was an out-of-body encounter and not just a remote view. In a way, this experience served as a kind of 'final exam' in my ambassador course, testing how I would react to a totally unexpected experience and an encounter with very different beings. I think I did pretty well."

For most of us, surrounded by a cluster of otherworldly beings that looked a lot like lobsters, it would seem a perfectly reasonable response to be intimidated; after all, fear of the unknown is a very primal and powerful emotion. Fortunately, Don Daniels is a great deal more open-minded than the average human being. He patiently allowed the little crustaceans to explore his body by touching him with their claws. It helped that he was receiving a very powerful sense of warmth, friendship, and unconditional love emanating from the extraterrestrials. Don was absolutely convinced that he was perfectly safe.

We will discuss Don's philosophy toward the UFO experience in a later chapter; for now, suffice it to say that he had spent the past few years building himself up to become an "ambassador to the universe." As part of that self-training, Don had taught himself to react positively toward extraterrestrial encounters, coming from a place of open-minded goodwill and curiosity rather than the more typical knee-jerk reaction of fear and suspicion and to consider the feelings and perspective of those he might meet.

One thing that may strike the reader of this book is just how different Don's extraterrestrial contact experiences have been in comparison to Al's. Al has spent a lifetime being tormented by the visitors, abducted against his will on countless occasions, and terrorized by the creatures that have made his life a veritable living hell. Don and Sierra, on the other hand, report almost entirely positive experiences, and when I asked them both about the reasons for this, they told me in a very matter-of-fact way that this could be put down to their having set boundaries or ground rules.

"I refuse to be involved with any entities whose motives are anything other than the best towards Earth and my fellow man," Don explains resolutely, "and with a couple of very rare exceptions, I have not attracted the attention of any of the darker entities that you hear so much about in the UFO field."

As I was in the process of researching this book and conducting interviews with many eyewitnesses and those who describe themselves as either abductees or contactees, I began to wonder just how much of this came down to perspective. Could Al and Don's experiences simply be two sides of the same coin, this marvel that we choose to call the UFO phenomenon?

Consider some of the darker, more terrifying UFO abduction experiences that are reported. A person is ripped from the warmth and safety of their home environment against their will. They are taken to a cold, sterile, almost clinical environment aboard an alien ship, where surgical procedures and tests are performed upon them—procedures that are uncomfortable (sometimes painful) and frightening in the extreme. They are often stripped naked. Once the abduction team has achieved their objectives (whatever those are) the poor abductee is returned to their home, sometimes indiscriminately dumped in the general vicinity, often with a huge chunk of time excised from their brain.

No wonder the experience is so terrifying.

I make my living as a paramedic, responding to 911 calls in order to treat those who are critically sick and injured. Consider this hypothetical case: You are a person from a less technologically developed culture, say some long-lost Amazonian rain forest tribe, and are somehow suddenly transported onto a remote stretch of road in the middle of back country modern-day America. Confused and disoriented, you stagger into the nearest road, where you are unfortunately hit by a car traveling at high speed.

911 is called. A paramedic such as myself arrives in an ambulance (in other words, a strange craft) with flashing rotating lights and sirens that make an unearthly wail. My EMT partner and I jump out. We look incredibly strange to you, dressed in bizarrely luminous clothing made of plastics, metals, and other materials that you have never seen before. You are in pain from your injuries, and are now terrified because of these two strange people who are already going about the business of abducting you (putting you on the wheeled gurney and loading you into the back of our ambulance).

Once there, the strange people cut off all of your clothes, leaving you as naked as the day you were born. You start to shiver, feeling cold and vulnerable, and cannot understand the strange language that the two people are speaking as they lean across your body, poking and prodding it mercilessly in an attempt to cause you more pain (actually, we are assessing the extent of your injuries).

The pain intensifies as sharp metal objects are poked into your body (an IV is started, so that we can give fluids in order to keep up your blood pressure and attempt to keep you alive). Sometimes bloods are extracted from the same IV line into vacutainer tubes for lab analysis, our own form of field medical experimentation. The salt water going into your vein through the IV is cold and leaves a strange taste in your mouth.

An oxygen mask is put over your face, shutting out part of the world around you and making you feel claustrophobic. Machines that flash lights and beep angry noises are stuck to your body (we're running an EKG in order to keep an eye on your heart, and monitoring the amount of oxygen saturating your bloodstream) and sometimes squeeze your arm so hard that it hurts (we're checking your blood pressure).

If things get really bad, we might be forced to insert a plastic breathing tube into your throat, making you gag and feel violated, but in reality also helping to maintain a patent airway and deliver precious oxygen to your traumatized cells.

Suddenly the "craft" stops, the back doors are flung open, and we are taking you out to somewhere even more unfamiliar . . . and every bit as frightening. Harsh neon lights pass by overhead as you float through the air on our wheeled gurney, taking corners at high speed until you arrive in a room full of people wearing similarly strange garb to that of the paramedics. Although you do not understand the concept, they are an emergency room team, highly skilled and possessed of one single overriding motive: to keep you alive, stabilize you, and hopefully restore you back to some semblance of your former health.

When looked at from the viewpoint of ignorance, the experience that I have just described would be a terrifying one. It is full of pain, fear, vulnerability, and humiliation. Unless you understood the motives of the paramedics and the ER team, you would feel abused and violated by their actions. But with just a little understanding of what these highly trained medical professionals are doing—and perhaps more importantly, why they are doing it—you will see the experience in an entirely different light, one that is all about your own best interests.

I cannot help but wonder if the UFO abduction experience isn't something every bit as dual-faceted. Unfortunately for us, most of us lack the frame of reference to understand the experience in its proper context . . . and so we are afraid.

In order to travel the vast interstellar distances between solar systems, or to use interdimensional means of crossing those same gulfs, the extraterrestrial visitors must by definition be significantly more advanced than human beings are. That is not to say that they are more advanced than we are spiritually, for some (such as the Greys) seem to behave in a manner that is amoral and bordering on the downright cruel; but others (such as the Nordics) do appear to have the very best of intentions toward humanity, acting in the furtherance of our global health and prosperity. (For more on this, see Dr. Michael Salla's books, *Getting to Yes with ET* and *Insiders Reveal Secret Space Programs and Extraterrestrial Alliances.*)

Might all of this truly be a matter of perspective?

Might our own limited perspective as human beings be more akin to that of the tribal stranger in a strange land than that of the paramedics who come to answer his distress call?

When it comes to the Greys, Don subscribes to the view put forward by the channeled being, Bashar: rather than being extra-terrestrials, Bashar claims that they are in fact the inhabitants of a parallel Earth, one that underwent an environmental catastrophe of epic proportions. Genetically similar to us, the Greys are motivated by the desire to interbreed human beings with their own kind, as they have lost the ability to reproduce biologically themselves; their ultimate goal is believed to be the creation of a hybrid human-Grey species, containing the best genetic features of each. If that is the case, then the purpose of an abduction in which the abductee is taken by the Greys may well be to collect genetic material in order to further this interbreeding project.

They are also said to have lost the ability to feel any kind of emotion, which may explain why they are perceived as being cold, calculating, and clinical by those people who have interacted with them—they display an almost sociopathic willingness to do whatever it takes to get the job done, no matter the collateral damage. After speaking to contactees and reviewing the literature of the ufology field, it does seem very clear that not only do the Greys have their own agenda, but also that they are utterly unconcerned with the feelings and well-being of the individual humans that end up as part of their experiment. One is forced to wonder whether this lack of concern extends to the future of the entire human race . . .

Don points out that the Greys may in fact serve as a cautionary tale, one that all of humanity would do well to heed. If they do indeed come from a parallel Earth, one in which their spirituality was outpaced by their development and acquisition of technology, then the end result was a devastating one for their species. Could we be on a similar path even as we speak, as we blithely destroy the environment and plunder the Earth's natural resources in exchange for little more than hollow material wealth? Might it be possible that, somewhere down the line, we could end up becoming them?

The very thought should make us shudder.

Having read Al's terrifying accounts of his interactions with the Reptilians, it was with no small sense of trepidation that I asked Don about them. Shaking his head, he told me that he had never encountered such a race of beings himself, although that does not rule out their existence. Nor has he encountered any "soulless" Greys, Reptillians, Praying Mantises, or other similarly negative extraterrestrial beings during his many years of interaction. Once again, this is not to say that such beings do not exist; Don attributes his lengthy track record of good experiences to the positive mindset that he always maintains during contact, and strict adherence to the rule that he will only work with beings of the highest moral and ethical values. So far, it has never steered him wrong.

In Don's world-view, reality exists in multiple dimensional layers of energy, each vibrating at a different frequency. The higher the vibrational frequency, the more likely that particular dimension is to be inhabited by or accessible to the more advanced extraterrestrial races, who are creatures of light and, therefore, much more comfortable in such an environment. Our Earth plane, on the other hand, is a world of relative doom, gloom, and darkness by comparison, and although the extraterrestrials can descend from the lighter upper dimensions in order to interact with humanity in this one, it is a laborious and rather unpleasant process for them.

I found this concept fascinating when Don explained it to me, because as a paranormal investigator of twenty years' standing, I have heard the afterlife and the spirit world explained in a very similar way. Numerous psychic mediums and authors have reported that the more enlightened, advanced, and plain old "good" a spirit or soul is, the greater their vibrational frequency tends to be, and, therefore, the higher level of dimension that they will occupy. Such spirits are capable of lowering themselves to our somewhat turgid vibrational level, but once again, the process is time-consuming and distasteful for them.

Don advocates a path toward spiritual enlightenment and light work as a means toward communicating with our "extraterrestrial cousins" in the upper dimensions. He hastens to point out that there is no one single tried and true method of increasing one's personal vibrational level to help meet the visitors halfway, and there is no one spiritual or religious path that is the "one true way." The roads toward becoming a cosmic citizen are many and varied, with numerous side-steps and branches.

One who claimed to be such a highly evolved soul was a lady who went by the name of Tashina. Don's first impression of Tashina was that she was perhaps a little on the shy side, for she spoke little and listened much more; but gradually he gave in to the nagging instinct, which was telling him that there was far more to Tashina's story than might first seem apparent.

The truth was finally revealed when Tashina told him that, "Earth is a very difficult assignment!" Tashina was no UFO contactee/abductee at all; rather, she claimed to be one of those advanced extraterrestrials herself, hailing from the planet Arcturus. She told Don that she had been dispatched here on a secret mission of no small importance and was in search of a facilitator to help her make her way in mainstream human society. Don would turn out to be that facilitator.

Nor was Tashina alone. She revealed to Don that there are literally millions of extraterrestrial visitors just like her at that time (two million in 2013, when things really heated up, and now one or two hundred thousand), living amongst us, hiding in plain sight, as we go about the business of our everyday lives. Most are volunteers sent here to help, to guide humanity and help us face the many challenges and obstacles that must be overcome; although they cannot fight our battles for us they are, at least, very much on our side, acting as cheerleaders from the sidelines. In much the same way as human beings might venture out on a mission to help the sick and destitute in Africa, such compassionate extraterrestrials undertake to do the same for us. After all, by their standards, we truly are spiritually destitute, no matter how advanced we might like to think we are.

As Don and Tashina communicated via the Internet, a most remarkable thing happened to his cat, El. Sadly, El developed a series of tumors, and the prognosis was bleak: She had breast cancer. Don and Terry are animal lovers to the core, and would do anything to take care of their fur babies, and so of course, surgery was scheduled as soon as possible in order to excise the tumors. Yet on the day that the surgery was due to take place, the vet found herself utterly astonished to find out that El's tumors were simply . . . gone.

El and Tashina had become firm friends during the course of the past few months, and when asked, Tashina admitted to having healed El herself via the medium of energy work. One of our interviews took place at Don's home, and I was introduced to El personally; she did indeed seem completely healed, wending her way through the kitchen and rubbing up against my leg in a blatant play for attention that was a pleasure to witness.

Who says miracles don't happen?

CHAPTER 8.

STAR CHILD

Much like Al, whose extraterrestrial contact experiences have been detailed elsewhere within these pages, Sierra Neblina believes that she deliberately chose to answer the Earth's call for help, and came here in order to help guide the planet and its inhabitants through a period of great spiritual turmoil and strife—albeit one that will hopefully result in an explosive growth of consciousness and enlightenment.

When I sat down to interview Sierra, I was presented with a graceful and erudite lady who laughs readily and is always ready to interject an insight or fascinating anecdote. She was unfailingly kind and polite during the hours we spent talking, along with fellow author and contactee Don Daniels. One would never guess that a little over a quarter century ago, Sierra was serving her country in the capacity of a Patriot missile battery driver (the Patriot was the US Army's principle ground-to-air missile, used for downing enemy aircraft and missiles) who was also trained as a sniper, not to mention highly skilled in hand-to-hand combat. When I learned this, I reminded myself fervently to not get on her bad side.

Ever since she was a young girl, Sierra was gifted with enhanced extrasensory abilities. More often than not, her dreams would come true, becoming nocturnal windows into events that had not yet come to pass. She also possessed natural healing abilities that were far beyond what most people would consider to be normal. She was naturally empathic, and seemed able to perceive and communicate with the spirits of those who had passed on.

Later on in life, Sierra enlisted in the US Army, eventually deploying to the Persian Gulf in 1990, as a part of Operation Desert Storm. As for so many veterans of that particular conflict—an estimated 250,000 out of the almost 700,000 who deployed—Sierra's service to her country was to exact a dreadful physical toll in the form of Desert Storm Syndrome (also known as Gulf War Syndrome).

Sierra was soon to undergo another transformative experience, when she woke in the early hours of the morning to find that something was amiss in her Colorado Springs bedroom: Not only was her partner absent, but an extraterrestrial being was standing there at the foot of her bed, simply watching her. It was one of the Greys, of whom we have already heard so much. No more than three feet high, the being seemed to be somehow capable of paralyzing Sierra, for despite her best efforts, she could not move a muscle.

She was then subjected to some kind of medical exam, which the Grey conducted in a totally calm and professional manner, in the style of a clinician who had obviously done this many times before. As the examination continued, Sierra became increasingly convinced that this was not the first time she had found herself in this particular situation, although she could not actively remember any contacts like it happening before. It is fair to say that most of us would have been terrified halfway out of our wits if we had found ourselves in the situation that Sierra did, but the Grey was helping to keep her calm by sending out soothing and reassuring telepathic messages directly into her mind.

By the time her experience was over, Sierra was relieved beyond measure to regain control of her motor function once more. Her arms and legs moved when she asked them to. Yet she could scarcely believe her eyes when she found out how long the Grey's examination had taken: over *four hours*. Sierra's missing partner stumbled back into the bedroom, having spent the last four hours in the bathroom without being consciously aware of it.

Wanting answers in the aftermath of her experience, Sierra reached out to a friend of hers who possessed psychic abilities. To say that the answer that her friend offered came as quite a shock would be a massive understatement. "Sierra," the friend said after giving her the once-over, "you're pregnant."

If so, Sierra told her, then it would have to have been an immaculate conception, because she was a lesbian. There was no potential father in this picture that could have contributed the necessary components to any pregnancy. Nonetheless, her friend stood her ground, insisting that the pregnancy was a very real thing. Determined to get to the bottom of the mystery, Sierra went to the store and invested in a bunch of home pregnancy testing kits.

They all came back positive. Each and every one.

Stunned by the news, Sierra nevertheless quickly began to adjust to the idea of becoming a mother. Weeks passed. Once every month or so, she would take another pregnancy test, just to be sure. Each was positive. Her abdomen began to expand noticeably. This was for real.

Four months after the first positive test, Sierra awoke and realized that something had changed, although she couldn't quite put her finger on what it was. Then, absently resting a hand on her abdomen, she quite literally *did* put her finger on it: Her belly was much flatter than it had been the day before. It was almost as if she had lost some form of bodily mass in the night. But that could only mean—

Hurriedly, she tried another pregnancy test. This time, for the first time in months, the strip came back negative. There had been no miscarriage, no spontaneous bleeding, or any kind of medical emergency that might explain the sudden reversal. She had simply gone to bed one evening being four months' pregnant, and awoken the next morning not pregnant at all.

It should have been a physical impossibility, yet nonetheless, there it was.

Struggling to come to terms with the sudden loss, Sierra reacted not with grief, but with anger. It was a productive anger, one that drove her to conduct research into the connection between the United States military and the extraterrestrial abduction phenomenon. Unfortunately, as many Ufologists and contactees have found out—sometimes to their detriment—when one takes an interest in the military and extraterrestrials, they will often take an interest right back in you.

Such was the case when, on returning home one evening, Sierra arrived to find a black four-door sedan parked in the driveway. Its inhabitants could not have been more classic Men in Black archetypes if they walked straight out of the movies. Wasting no time, one of the MIBs gruffly told her to get into the car.

Today (writing this in 2016), the Cheyenne Mountain Complex (CMC) is used as a training facility, and as a backup control center in case disaster strikes. During the nineties, when Sierra was ordered to get into the limo and was subsequently driven there, CMC was the home to NORAD whose job was to ever-vigilantly scan the skies above the US and Canada, keeping a watchful eye out for intruding enemy aircraft, incoming missiles . . . and who knows what else. For those (like the author) who are fans of science fiction in all its various forms, Cheyenne Mountain is also where they keep the eponymous device from the movie and TV series *Stargate*.

This secretive complex was blasted and burrowed out of the mountainside during the 1960s, by a combined group of US Army engineers and private contractors. To say that the facility is highly robust would be an understatement: It is designed to withstand everything but a direct hit from a thermonuclear weapon.

After the requisite security checks, the black four-door sedan was waved through the various gates and guard posts, until Sierra was finally taken into the interior of the Cheyenne Mountain Complex itself. Sierra's MIB escort introduced her to a scientist, who was about to challenge the way in which human beings understood the laws of physics to work.

The scientist proceeded to demonstrate a device that sounds like, to all intents and purposes, a transporter, as seen on the TV show *Star Trek*. It actually looked like a large coffee maker, which had a place where the operator could raise a transparent shield to encase a soda can. He used it to teleport that soda can from one side of the room to the other, where it rematerialized in a sealed chamber.

Suspicious of this being some form of trickery, the scientist scratched an "X" shape into the can and challenged the Sierra to watch closely as he repeated the process. He did so, and the newly scarred can once again made the journey from one side of the room to the other. Quite why she had been brought here to be shown such advanced technology, Sierra had no idea.

Events took an even more bizarre turn when the black-suited men who had brought her there in the limousine escorted her on a tour of some of the complex's hidden treasures. One such chamber contained the body of a tall, gray alien, which she estimated to be some six feet in height. It appeared to be dead, and had been laid out on a table. Any thoughts that she might have had of touching the creature were stymied when she realized that it was enclosed in a protective glass case.

The next stop on her tour allowed the MIB to show off some kind of gravity-defying flying craft, which hovered silently a few feet above the ground. Sierra was being given a guided tour of some of the US government's most tightly guarded secrets. The question remained: Why?

That question would be answered at the end, when she was escorted to a conference room and ushered into a seat. After a long wait that she had no way of actually measuring, an older man came in to speak with her. Sierra estimated that he was in his fifties, and was intrigued to see that the flight suit he wore bore absolutely no markings of rank or insignia whatsoever—absolutely no clues to his unit affiliation or identity. Except, the flight suit he wore was the navy colors, not the air force colors, which confused Sierra.

Without preamble, the man told her that she had now gotten the answers she had been looking for (presumably he meant those regarding the reality of the UFO phenomenon) and that she had, therefore, better stop digging. Although she was no longer an actively serving soldier, Sierra had remained in the Army Reserves, and really had little choice but to follow orders. Over the following months, she backed off almost entirely from her research into the realm of the extraterrestrial.

She still had no idea what had become of her unborn child.

A Kindred Relationship

It would be many years later that Sierra met and struck up a friendship with Don, a kindred spirit to whom she could turn for support when it came to her extraterrestrial experiences. She was becoming increasingly convinced that somewhere out there, the child she had never met (nor carried to full term) was calling out to her, wanting to make contact with its long-lost mother.

Don is a proponent of the theory that those human beings who find themselves abducted by the Greys and other races are actually willing participants, having signed a "soul contract" to do so before they incarnated in human form. Over dinner one night, Don and Sierra discussed the possibility of such a soul contract being modifiable by the person who had made it. Was such a thing possible, or was the contract figuratively "set in stone?"

Sierra resolved to find out. Not wanting to trash the contract entirely, she focused her mind and sent out the express intention that from then on, she would only consent to work with those extraterrestrial races and factions who operated with good and noble intent. This line of thinking had worked for Don in the past, he told her, and it turned out that it worked very well for Sierra, too. After that mental "letter of intent" was sent out to the cosmos, never again did she have contact with some of the more unsavory varieties of extraterrestrial visitors.

Yet still the feeling of her long-lost child wanting to make contact remained. Sierra was sure that she could sense a male presence, invisible but very tangibly *there,* in her bedroom, whenever she retired for the night. She felt convinced that it was her child. Despite her very best efforts, the presence remained frustratingly just beyond her reach.

Don, on the other hand, was convinced for some indefinable reason that Sierra had borne a daughter, not a son. He communicated as much in an email to her, but she remained unmoved, still certain that the male presence in her bedroom was the son she had never seen. Don decided to try and resolve the impasse by talking with Tashina, asking her if she could shed any light on the situation.

As things turned out, Don was correct. Tashina was able to establish contact with Sierra's daughter, who proceeded to manifest physically at Tashina's house in an almost-ethereal form composed of pure energy. The visitor explained that she was meant to be a bridge between Earth and the cosmos, a mission that she had been chosen to undertake and had willingly accepted. She had been given the rather remarkable opportunity of selecting her own mother, and Sierra had been her choice. This information (and a whole lot more) was relayed during the course of a long phone conversation between Tashina and Sierra, after which things would progress to the next step: Sierra would get to meet her daughter at last.

So who was the male presence that Sierra had sensed in her bedroom? It transpired that a spiritually advanced entity had come forward to act in a role similar to that of a "spirit guide," helping to prepare the ground for Sierra's first contact with her daughter.

This was to be no face-to-face meeting, however—thanks to her natural abilities, Sierra was able to somehow internally host her daughter's energy form, allowing it to manifest within her and (for want of a better term) share the same headspace. It felt almost as if the two were on a joint astral journey together, one that was as wildly disorientating as any roller coaster. Although Sierra's body wasn't going anywhere, her consciousness was traveling fast, hand in hand with that of her child.

Sierra had jotted down notes as she journeyed, hoping that they would be legible and useful once she returned. The notes actually read like a conversation between two separate individuals, almost as if somebody had listened in and transcribed their chat from start to finish. This was almost certainly a variation of automatic writing, the technique employed by psychic mediums in order to channel the spirits of the dead and allow them to express themselves via the medium of the written word (although skeptics will argue that it is simply the writer's own subconscious that is guiding the pen or pencil across the page).

The joining lasted from midnight until dawn the following day, almost seven hours in duration. Sierra paid the price, spending the next few days laid up and recuperating from what turned out to be quite a severe infection. Had the physiologic stress of the event overwhelmed Sierra's immune system, rendering her susceptible to an opportunistic virus? Whether or not that turned out to be the case, it was a price that she was glad to have paid, in exchange for one precious night with her long-lost little girl.

CHAPTER 9.

NOT OF
THIS WORLD

There are some opportunities in life that you just can't pass up. I had both heard and read a great deal about Tashina from Don and Sierra, as you've learned. She tended to shun the spotlight, keeping a very low profile and traveling on a regular basis, and very much liked to keep to herself. On occasion, I heard that she would visit a convention here and a seminar there, but her location at any given time was known to very few people.

When Don told me that he had spoken with her about this book project and that she had agreed to an interview, I jumped at the chance. After all, how often does one get to speak with a person who may not have been born on the same planet as we have?

The tentative plan was for Tashina and I to meet in person, as I much prefer conducting face-to-face interviews when possible. They're more relaxed and less formal than the other methods of interviewing, I like to think. Yet there was a problem: Tashina was currently embroiled in a dangerous situation and would be unable to come and meet me prior to the book's publishing deadline.

As I write these words in the winter of 2016, the eyes of America (and much of the rest of the world) are turned toward what is officially being called the "Dakota Access Pipeline," an 1,172-mile conduit that is under construction across several states. Intended to funnel oil underground from North Dakota to a storage facility in Illinois, the route of the pipeline brings it directly through lands that have long been held sacred by several Native American tribes, who are understandably concerned about the impact that the oil will have on their natural environment—particularly the water.

Having first tried to oppose the pipeline through conventional channels (which were predictably rebuffed), the people of the Standing Rock Sioux tribe eventually moved to more tangible means of protest, establishing a camp to which thousands of supporters would subsequently flock from all across the country.

Strong-arm tactics employed by private security guards and some law enforcement agencies generated even greater support for the protesters, and media coverage of the events swelled their ranks even further. Tashina felt moved to offer her services and was making her way to Standing Rock as quickly as she could, helping to feed the men and women, educate the children of the camp, and tend to their injuries. This was by no means a new thing for her; Tashina had worked with a relief agency in the aftermath of Hurricane Katrina.

The weather at Standing Rock was extremely cold (made worse when water cannons were used against the protestors), and the conditions were austere. Nevertheless, she kindly took a few hours out of her journey to find an area with cell phone reception and carry out a long-distance interview with me. While I sat in the comfortable surroundings of my home office in Colorado, secure in the warmth as I took down notes during our conversation, I could only wince at the privations that Tashina and her fellow protestors must be enduring.

I had been thinking about the interview a great deal in advance of it actually taking place. Claiming to have originated on a distant world is no small thing, and I knew that many people would simply pooh-pooh the very possibility without giving it any serious consideration. For my part, as a writer and paranormal investigator who was used to dealing with extraordinary claims, I knew that I had to proceed on the assumption that she was indeed telling the truth, to the very best of her knowledge.

What questions would *you* ask of such a person? Where do you even *begin?*

When I picked up the phone and started up my digital voice recorder, the first thing that struck me was the timbre of Tashina's voice. It was mellifluous and light, seeming to rise barely above the level of a whisper, and also had an unusual cadence the likes of which I had never really heard before.

We began with a confirmation on Tashina's part that she was indeed Arcturian in origin, and had intentionally chosen to visit the Earth at one of the most tumultuous points in its history, in order to help out its inhabitants as much as she possibly could, in the same way than an American might choose to volunteer to join the Peace Corps in order to bring relief to those less fortunate who are living overseas. In this case, the "overseas" in question was simply several orders of magnitude bigger!

I asked specifically about the nature of the help that she was here to bring: Was it to educate, perhaps, to expand awareness; or was there an element of helping to raise the positive energy of the planet, as several contactees had told me during earlier interviews?

"That's very basic and an oversimplification," she chided me gently. Knowing that I was a paramedic by chosen profession, she continued, "When you go into somebody's home in response to an emergency, you do far more than simply educate or try to raise some kind of energy, don't you?" I said I agreed. "You use various skill sets in order to make the situation better, in addition to just the basics. It's the same way for me."

When I pointed out that a paramedic tends to work one-on-one with individual patients, for the most part, I then asked whether she did the same thing or worked with larger groups. She laughed and said that it was an excellent question. "The answer is that I do both. You have to remember that people are *people,* not objects. Each one has a story to tell, and each one has his or her own unique set of needs and gifts. I want to know 'who are you?' in each case. Meeting with them one-on-one allows me to appreciate that and build a relationship, but I can then scale up to see each of them as part of the larger whole. Each one has to know that they matter; that they count; that they're *important.*"

She was actually talking about a subject that is very dear to my heart, and also that of many medical professionals: the importance of cultivating a bedside manner, thinking of the patient as a human being first and foremost, rather than as a disease process or an injury pattern.

How many more beings of a similar nature to Tashina are living here on the Earth, working toward the same purpose? A great many, she responded. They were all here to offer their assistance in as many ways as they possibly could, with the greater goal of helping to elevate the human race out of its current precarious situation—a hole that we have essentially dug for ourselves.

Fascinated by the direction that our conversation was taking, I asked about the global picture. Was humanity making progress in a positive direction, or were things really as bleak as the twenty-four-hour news media liked to suggest?

"Positive progress is being made," she confirmed, and went on to tell me that an increasingly large number of people are present on Earth who are spiritually aware and enlightened, acting as beacons of positive energy, like lighthouses around which a great storm was raging. By her own admission, Tashina liked to speak by way of analogy. She described this as being a very dark time for the Earth, and when one looked at the spiritual, moral, political, and environmental state of affairs, it was very easy to see exactly what she meant. "The wrong people have been put in positions of power, and there's going to have to be a clean-up. We can't throw out the baby with the bath water and condemn all the people of the Earth for the actions of a few morally bankrupt individuals." [[A *few*? Cough. Sorry.]]

That made a great deal of sense to me, and echoed what Don and Sierra had explained during my interviews with them.

"So what is to be done about it?" Tashina asked, somewhat rhetorically. "You call in the galactic equivalent of the United Nations . . . and that's who *we* are. You cannot do this alone. It has gone too far. It's too massive. You need our help."

Intrigued, I asked whether that meant that the "Galactic UN" was here to level the playing field. I was starting to introduce a few analogies of my own.

"You need a referee, and you need peacekeepers, all of whom are capable of looking at the bigger picture. Wherever you see a great emergency, you will see *us*. But once the emergency is over and the clearing-up has started, we'll look at the root cause and help make sure that something on this scale is never allowed to happen again. It's not as if we can keep coming in every time humanity has a crisis and helping to fix it for you."

I paused for a moment to reflect on that. Once again, it made sense. Let's look at the "bigger picture" as it relates to everyday international politics for us here on Earth. When there's a crisis on the global stage, there are a number of options for sending help; foreign aid is a wonderful thing. But there are only so many times that most governments are willing to "send in the Marines" before a more permanent solution needs to be found, otherwise it's basically putting a Band-Aid on a festering open wound.

"It's only once people's basic needs are met, that they are safe, protected, and well-fed, that you can really begin to educate and address the root cause of the problem. You don't educate a woman in the middle of giving birth to a baby in the finer points of contraception!" she laughed. "We're in the process of taking care of basic human needs right now and trying to set up safe zones. *Then* we can get into raising the frequency of human energies. Do you follow?"

I thought that I did, but there was one thing I didn't understand. "This is an age-old question," I began carefully, hoping not to cause offense, "but why don't you just land on the White House lawn, announce your presence to the world, and say, 'Here we are? Now let's get to work?' Why the cloak of secrecy?"

To my mind, that was the million-dollar question. Wouldn't most of humanity's problems disappear practically overnight if extraterrestrials revealed themselves and told us to basically knock it off, and get our priorities straightened out?

"We *have* landed on the White House lawn," she chuckled, and went on to mention the case of Valiant Thor, a man who was believed by many to have been a Venusian extraterrestrial; 'Val,' as he liked to be known, was said to have secretly met with both President Dwight D. Eisenhower and Vice President Richard Nixon, spending time at both the White House and the Pentagon. She also mentioned the incident at Rendlesham Forest in Great Britain, where a UFO is said to have landed in the woods just outside a United States airbase—a landing that was witnessed by numerous officers and enlisted men sent to investigate it. "There's no real secret here. There are so many documented cases of contact from around the world and throughout history, if you know where to look."

Leaning back in my chair, I swiveled to look at my office bookshelves. They were practically groaning under the weight of my UFO book collection. I had always wanted to know precisely how much of the material contained within those books was genuine, and how much was pure fiction. There were stories of close encounters, abductions, genetic experimentation, secret space programs, and hundreds of extraterrestrial races. There was no way that it could *all* be true, but just how much of it was genuine? I decided to ask.

"Quite a bit is either misunderstanding or misrepresentation," Tashina explained. "I've been to a number of UFO conferences, and I've found the misinformation to be found at some of them to be shocking. It's why I rarely speak at those kinds of events, except in cases where a portion of the proceeds are donated to charity. Too many people have an 'on-planet view,' when they should have an 'off-planet view,' as we do. Things look very different when you are no longer Earthbound. It's not that these people are deliberately lying, in most cases, or deliberately giving misinformation; it's simply that they have a very narrow worldview, a limited picture instead of the whole thing. Through no fault of their own, they lack perspective . . . but they write about it as if they're an authority."

Hearing that last sentence, I was glad that I had openly professed my ignorance on the subject of ufology at the beginning of my own work in progress that you are now holding in your hands.

"We don't want to cause fear," Tashina went on. "It paralyses people, stops them from thinking clearly, and landing on the White House lawn as you put it would serve to create a lot of fear! We only interact with people in places where there will be no fear. The contact sessions that people like Don are a part of do not create fear either."

Tashina added that her fellow extraterrestrial volunteers are currently meeting with people all across the planet, landing their ships in out-of-the-way locations and making contact with those who are ready to interact with them in a positive manner.

"We're not like you. If you want to meet with us in our spacecraft, then a great deal of education is necessary in order for you to do that. It would be *devastating* for you to have that type of interaction with us on an ongoing basis if you weren't prepared—without the proper raising of your vibrations. All of the things that you have heard about where we are concerned are just the tip of the iceberg. Very few of you are prepared to handle an encounter with us in our full forms. It would shock you very badly."

I turned the conversation toward the relatively recent proliferation of extraterrestrial contact in the mainstream media and popular culture. *Close Encounters of the Third Kind; E.T. The Extra-Terrestrial; Star Trek; The X-Files;* so many films, television shows, and books have portrayed versions of such encounters that they are now firmly rooted in the fabric of modern culture. I asked whether this was deliberate, an intentional "softening-up" of the public in order to better facilitate their acceptance of actual contact when it did indeed take place. She said that it was.

"It's part of the preparation that is required in order for people to come into sustained contact with us, in the same way that a deep sea diver or an astronaut has to prepare before they enter a harsh environment. It involves training those people to be emotionally prepared, physically prepared, spiritually prepared, and of course, *psychologically* prepared! Think of it like this: Somebody can be extremely intelligent, yet psychologically unable to stand a long flight on an airplane. It's not a question of intelligence when the mind and body rebel against the process of flying. So it is when it comes down to contact with us. Anybody wanting to connect with us has to come from a place of spirituality, with pure motives that come from the heart."

Another question of great import that I wanted to ask involved religion. Although I am an agnostic myself, I really wanted to know whether any of the Earth's orthodox religions had truly "gotten it right."

"Not one," Tashina responded without hesitation. "They all have one thing in common: They acknowledge a higher source, which is correct, but unfortunately they have taken that concept and tried to shove it into a box, tried to bottle it by giving it various different terms according to whichever culture or geographic region they arose from. Most of them have been used as social control mechanisms throughout history."

Something else that had fascinated me about Tashina's story ever since Don had told me about her was the idea of her being physically different to those people who were born and raised on Earth and came from plain old human genetic stock.

"I have been thoroughly assessed by a well-respected physicist, and he was unable to properly analyze my DNA. My physical makeup seems to be beyond human understanding, and he was unable to satisfactorily explain quite how my extraordinary body does some of the extraordinary things that it does, such as healing."

I should point out that coming from many people, such a statement might sound arrogant; coming from Tashina, however, it seemed quite the opposite. During our entire conversation, not once did she sound anything but humble and matter-of-fact.

As Don had said previously, Tashina appeared to have the ability to heal (cats, in addition to people!) over long distances, sometimes with little more than a phone call as a connective medium.

"Being a healer is part of my natural state, my natural being. It's who and what I am, and I don't tend to give it much conscious thought. I'm here on Earth to heal and to protect. It can take a great toll on me, and so I often need to 'retreat' for lack of a better word, in order to regroup and recharge my energies. I don't take energy from others, you see; I'm more like a generator that creates energy for other people to use."

At that point, it was time for us both to go our separate ways. Tashina had given me a great deal of food for thought, raising questions that I still mull over to this day. Doubtless many people will dismiss her claims out of hand, writing them off as nothing more than fantasies of the imagination. But consider for a moment how much of what she has to say makes sense to *you,* personally. Ignore what anybody else might think, and simply consider things from her perspective.

Does the world truly need a "galactic UN" and an army of spiritually advanced volunteers to intervene in our present situation? Turn on PBS, CNN, the BBC, or whichever news media outlet seems least biased to you. Look at the state of the world.

Are her claims *really* so far-fetched? I leave that for the reader to decide.

CHAPTER 10.

FIELD TRIP

The result of my interviews with Don and Sierra had been fascinating, but they had also left me with at least as many questions as they had answered. For example, some of the claims that they were making were quite literally out of this world. I wondered if there was some way in which they could be verifiably tested.

When I broached the subject with them both, they came up with a great idea: Would I be interested in joining them on a field trip? Don, Sierra, and a few trusted others would undertake them regularly, heading out to an isolated part of the country at sundown with nothing more than some folding chairs and a flashlight each. They were part of a long-running working group that was employing meditative states and the technique known as remote viewing on a fairly frequent basis.

The intent was simple. If the conditions were right and everything aligned properly, they told me, then it was sometimes possible for contact to be established with some of the extraterrestrial visitors that may be passing through our little corner of the galactic neighborhood.

I figured that we had nothing to lose, and so I gratefully accepted their offer. We arranged to meet at Don's home on a night in November when all of us were free.

Don warned me about my mindset in advance. "We are amping up the seriousness level a lot each year," he explained, "and I want you all to be comfortable with whatever might happen. If you are still wrapped up in the Fear Paradigm, *you* need to do some serious introspection. If you are worried about being 'abducted,' then that is the level of vibration that you are putting out, and that is what you will attract. That is *not* where we want to be, or what we want to attract. There is plenty of peaceful interaction going on, and if you have raised your consciousness to that higher level and are *living* the Peaceful Paradigm, *that* is what you will attract, and that is where the group has to be for this to happen."

I tried to bear this philosophy in mind when the night of the excursion arrived. In addition to the basics for spending a few hours out in the middle of nowhere at night, I packed a few items of specialist equipment— mostly things that I employed in my role as a paranormal investigator, such as a digital voice recorder.

Perhaps the most useful piece of equipment was a FLIR: a forward-looking infra-red camera, essentially a heat-sensing camera. Once the exclusive province of the military, thermal imaging technology had come down drastically in price, until it was relatively affordable for the guy or gal in the street. If there were any unexplained heat sources around that coming night, then the FLIR would pick them up. From a more prosaic point of view, it would also help rule out the presence of uninvited night-time visitors, such as nocturnal animals and pranksters of the human variety.

Although the daytime Colorado weather in November can be warm and pleasant, things are very different when the sun goes down. Temperatures plummet very quickly after dark. With this in mind, we all wrapped up warm in several layers of clothing before heading out.

Don took the wheel and drove us out into the hills outside of the city of Evergreen. The number of lights from nearby houses grew increasingly sparse, until finally we turned off onto a narrow, winding track that led onto some private land that was owned by a friend of Don's named Lance. Lance had a strong interest in the field of ufology, and was a regular attendee at the working groups. His parcel of land was hidden away from most prying eyes in a beautifully scenic little valley, with only a few scattered and distant neighbors.

When the three of us got out of Don's car, Lance introduced himself. Handshakes were exchanged all around. He was a friendly, effusive man, and I found myself warming to him immediately. With the exception of some very funky rock music drifting in from one of the far-off houses, the night was very still and quiet, with little in the way of wind to stir the branches and rustle the long grass.

Outlining the plan for the evening, it became very apparent that Don had done his homework, going so far as to identify the two passes that the International Space Station would make across the night skies above us that evening.

Trekking out into the center of a meadow, we set out four chairs in a square, and then sat down facing one another. Don and Sierra encouraged us to focus our attention on the universe, to broadcast our feelings of good intent and desire for contact with only the good, ethical extraterrestrial races of the galaxy, those that were willing to work with us for the betterment of humankind and the greater good.

I tilted my head back and gazed at the glorious panoply of stars arching over our heads. Assuming that Don, Sierra, and many of the people that I had interviewed for this book were correct, then that vast expanse of cosmic ocean was far from empty; rather, it was teeming with life, and some of that life had not only developed sufficiently advanced technologies to travel interstellar space, it was also aware of our presence and was willing to communicate with us.

How extraordinary a concept was *that?*

Minutes passed without anything apparently happening. Then Sierra broke the silence and said that there were a number of entities in the vicinity, and that they were open to our attempts to make contact with them.

"Turn on your cameras," Sierra instructed us, "and start taking pictures over in that direction." Obediently we complied, snapping a series of photographs of the valley's western slope. I couldn't see anything worth writing home about with the naked eye, but we kept shooting, trusting in her instincts and capabilities.

There were a number of extraterrestrial beings standing just inside the treeline, she informed us. When I asked what they were doing, she replied that they were simply observing us, apparently as curious about their human visitors as we were about them.

Without any warning at all, Sierra suddenly sprang up out of her chair and headed toward the line of trees where she said that she sensed the entities. After taking another string of photographs, I traded my basic camera for its FLIR variant. When I fired the device up, it flashed a "low battery" warning that made me frown. I had made a point of charging all of my electrical devices before leaving the house that night (I verified the charge on them all), and inserting factory fresh batteries into those that required them. There should be no reason for the FLIR to be ninety-percent drained of power; I hadn't even powered it on since checking that it was fully charged earlier that evening.

I took a few paces in Sierra's direction and made a sweep with the FLIR, putting particular emphasis on the treeline, which appeared dark and empty to the naked eye. I was fully expecting to find nothing unusual in thermal part of the spectrum, so you can probably imagine my surprise when I discovered a number of visual anomalies on the screen. When viewed through the "eye" of a thermal camera, the hotter an object is, the brighter white that it appears. The multiple objects that I was seeing on screen were pure white, making them far hotter than their surroundings. They would also move, appearing and disappearing, sometimes over the space of a few seconds, and sometimes remaining present for several minutes.

The only things that I had seen behave comparably on the FLIR were rocks, which soaked up the sunlight during the day, growing relatively warm, and then slowly discharging it when the temperature dropped at night. There were a few rocks and boulders to be found around the meadow, allowing me to use them as a point of comparison. They looked similar to the anomalies I was seeing over in the treeline, but the big difference was that *those* sources of warmth appeared to be floating in mid-air.

Sierra disappeared into the cover of the treeline. Lance, Don, and I went a little closer. The anomalies appeared to be fluctuating. When Sierra's own glowing white form reappeared ten minutes later, one of them expanded vertically to what we estimated was somewhere between twenty and thirty feet high.

Viewing the Evidence

When we returned to Don's house, the three of us uploaded our digital images onto his PC in order to view them on a larger monitor screen.

Sierra pointed to a number of what the ghost hunting community likes to call "orbs"—luminous points of semi-transparent light. They were all over our photographs. I cautioned them not to think of these particular light anomalies as being related to the extraterrestrial entities, however. Paranormal investigators had been running into them since the arrival of the affordable digital camera, I explained, and there was nothing mysterious about the vast majority of them; most were typically particles of dust, pollen, or dander, which was entirely to be expected when using flash photography in the middle of a meadow at night.

That's not to say that there weren't any photographic anomalies, however. Some fascinating things were revealed upon closer examination of the images. One photograph, taken with a basic camera and using a flash, had focused on me, sitting in my chair with my eyes closed (trying to preserve some night vision from the effects of the flash) and taking a photo of something else. I occupy the left third of the frame. On the right-hand side of the frame is a nebulous white mist, which seems to be leaning my direction. The same mist appears in a later photograph, taken from a different position. One of the possible explanations that a good paranormal investigator will look for when a photograph is taken outdoors in cold weather is that of the photographer's breath fogging the lens—however, none of the other photographs contained any comparable mists; nor were any of our group smokers, so cigarette smoke was also ruled out as a possible answer.

When I drove home from Don's house that evening, I kept turning the events of the field trip over in my mind, examining them from all angles. There hadn't been a Hollywood-style extraterrestrial spacecraft landing, but then again I hadn't really expected one. The photographic anomalies were interesting, and despite my best efforts to find an explanation for them in the days that followed, I was unable to explain them away. Nor were any of the fellow paranormal investigators that I showed them to.

Despite Sierra's assurances that we had been joined by extraterrestrial visitors, there was no concrete proof of that which could be offered to anybody. Most people would write off the unusual images as a camera malfunction or a naturally-occurring phenomenon.

Nonetheless, I found the experience to be a very spiritual one. Sitting there in the middle of the great outdoors in good company underneath the stars and contemplating our place in a much broader universe had made the trip well worth it. It broadened my perspective and primed me for my encounter with what was to be the final interviewee, a man who was both a much sought-after artist and an extraterrestrial abductee.

CHAPTER 11.

THE EXTRATERRESTRIAL ARTIST

Whether they choose to describe themselves as *experiencers, contactees,* or by the more sinister-sounding descriptor of *abductees,* one thing is undeniable: The effect that these extraordinary events have had upon their lives can run the entire gamut, ranging from the upbeat and positive to the destructive and negative.

Some have unfortunately fallen victim to substance abuse and the misery of addiction, in a desperate attempt to cope with the stresses and pressures of interacting with extraterrestrial races; others have reacted in the opposite way, seeing the experience in a positive light and using it to fuel their artistic talents.

One such man is Chuck Chroma. Chuck's chosen medium of creative expression is painting, and the Denver-based artist's unique brand of art is much in demand: His work has been exhibited in galleries across the country, exemplifying a style of art that he likes to refer to as *Southwestern Expressionism.* Landscapes, animals, and plants are a constant theme of Chuck's work, but there is also a far less conventional series of paintings that have been inspired by the artist's experiences as an abductee.

Chuck maintains that he has been abducted by extraterrestrial visitors ever since he was a very young boy, and although a selective amnesia seems to have been induced in order to cover them up, a hypnotherapist was successfully able to regress Chuck backward to key points in his life and recover what appear to be repressed memories. This therapy occurred at the age of forty-five, and those recovered memories have served as the inspiration for several of Chuck's favorite paintings.

"I feel fortunate not to have been abducted by the Reptilians," Chuck told me during our interview. "Although I have never encountered them directly, I have been told that those who experience contact with them find it to be very traumatic. There are instances of them causing a lot of emotional, psychological, and even *physical* damage."

Chuck was abducted by the Greys, who he describes as being more gentle and loving in nature than their Reptilian counterparts. His first experience began when a blinding white light came in through the window of his bedroom, awakening the four-year-old, who had been soundly sleeping on the top bunk. Fast asleep on the bottom bunk, his brother remained undisturbed as Chuck sat up in bed to discover with total astonishment that something akin to a tall, slender Praying mantis was standing at the foot of the bunk, gripping the bedpost as it watched him soundlessly.

"I've learned since that the Praying mantises are really in charge of the Greys, who are pretty much their helpers," he went on to explain, echoing what I had been told by several other contactees during other interviews. "There are different castes. Think of it like a hive, where you have worker bees, queens, and drones to carry out the various different tasks. The Greys are very insectoid in nature and have that hive-mind mentality, with the Praying mantises being the bosses."

The Mantis lifted Chuck out of bed and carried him into the light, which was streaming through the west-facing window, where he was then carried in the light beam up into the sky above his house and on into a craft.

Despite what could easily have been a terrifying experience, the young Chuck felt absolutely no fear at all, which is remarkable when one considers the circumstances—not even when the visitors peeled his clothes off and turned them inside-out. He described instead a sense of great wonder and amazement, another commonly related characteristic of the abduction experience.

He underwent some kind of medical examination, after which his clothes were given back to him, and then his abductors returned the young boy to his bed. The following morning, Chuck ran into the kitchen and excitedly told his mother about having been "visited by the balloon-headed people!"

Chuck's mother quite understandably dismissed the entire thing as a dream, the product of a young boy's vivid imagination. Yet abduction very often seems to run in families. When I asked Chuck about a potential familial connection with his parents, he revealed that it was many years later that he would learn about his father also being an abductee; his mother apparently was not. He believes that the same may also have been the case with his paternal grandfather or grandmother, and that the phenomenon is inter-generational in nature. I could not help but wonder just how far back this might have gone. Chuck also experienced being present on a ship with his father at one point, something that only came up during a hypnotic memory regression; to the best of Chuck's knowledge, his father was never consciously aware that he was an abductee.

The frequency of abductions increased significantly when he hit puberty, occurring on a very regular basis; he estimates the total for those years as being "dozens of times." The reason for this is something that we can only speculate about, but Chuck is an adherent to the belief that part of the visitors' agenda involves an inter-species breeding program, as we shall see shortly; with puberty being the age at which human beings become capable of reproduction, could this be the reason for the unearthly visitors taking a heightened interest in him?

On the Road

In *The Holy Ghost Hot Springs Abduction,* two heavy trucks race side-by-side along the highway, while an extraterrestrial (one of the classic black-eyed Greys) flies through the air in front of them, outlined against a dark, starry sky. A Volkswagen bus is parked at the side of the highway, next to a sign that reads "Holy Ghost."

The inspiration for this story dates back to a road trip vacation that Chuck took in 1985. Chuck had been reading a book about the various hot springs that were scattered around the state of New Mexico, and had decided to visit as many of them as he could, driving from site to site in his trusty '69 VW Bus.

North of Santa Fe on Highway 44 lay the Holy Ghost Hot Springs, Chuck's next intended vacation spot. When he spotted a sign by the side

of the road that read "Holy Ghost," he parked the truck next to it and set off to find the springs to take a look for himself. According to a guide book that he'd read on the subject, there had been an actual resort there once; it had burned all the way down to the foundations sixty years earlier, leaving nothing behind but rubble. The springs themselves were still there, but they were hardly appealing: pools of fetid water that stank of a combination of cow feces and sulfur.

With there being nothing else of interest for him to see, Chuck made his way back to the VW, ready to move on to his next stop. Hopping back behind the wheel, he was leafing through his guidebook, when suddenly he noticed two figures walking along the path that led from the hot springs toward the highway. It struck him as being a little odd that there should be foot traffic out here in the middle of nowhere; he had a clear view along the highway in both directions and couldn't see any parked cars.

Although it was difficult to make out any details, Chuck could see that the larger of the two figures was wearing a bright blue jacket. They both disappeared behind a tree. Chuck sat there watching them, waiting for them to come out from behind the tree so that he could get a better look at them.

They never reappeared. Chuck was afraid. The fear had come out of nowhere, with no apparent cause. In the space of just a few heartbeats, it had grown into full-blown terror.

He suddenly felt the bizarre compulsion to climb into the back of the bus and light a candle—strange indeed, given the fact that it was still broad daylight. But when the candle was lit, Chuck realized that he had placed it too close to the VW's roof interior, and it was now burning the lining. Hastily, he snuffed it out. Staring at the scorch mark curiously, he felt as though it was imbued with some sort of mystical significance, for lack of a better term, though he could not for the life of him say why.

Then the fear was back, gripping him like a panic attack. In an attempt to secure his safety, Chuck decided that it would be a good idea to lock all of the VW's doors. When he had done that, it dawned on him that it had suddenly gone from broad daylight to the darkness of night, seemingly in no time at all. The trucks flying past him on the highway now had their high-beams on.

He needed to get away. Turning the key, Chuck was horrified to discover that the engine was totally dead. There was nothing mysterious about that—the VW could be temperamental at the best of times—but now more than ever it was a huge pain in the butt, because now he would have to try and do a rolling start on the bus.

Before rolling out onto the highway in the darkness, he took a look both ways. The only set of oncoming headlights were quite some distance away, and would be in the opposite lane to the one that he would be reversing the Bus into. There was no traffic behind him in his own lane, and so he figured that it should be safe enough.

A voice that Chuck clearly heard inside his mind said, "Don't go, you are in danger."

He decided to trust the voice, sitting silently behind the wheel, determined not to do anything until he figured out the nature of the danger that the voice was warning him about.

It didn't take long for Chuck to find out exactly what the danger was.

The pair of oncoming headlights suddenly doubled, splitting in half as they rushed toward him. Chuck squinted in puzzlement. Finally, he realized what was happening: They were two eighteen-wheeler trucks, racing one another side-by-side as one driver attempted to overtake the other. Chuck watched with his mouth gaping as they blasted past him, occupying both lanes of the highway.

If he had backed his VW out into the nearest lane in order to try and start it, one of them would have hit him—at a good seventy-five miles per hour.

He would have been killed.

It wasn't until 1997 that Chuck would find out the entire story, thanks to a regression conducted by his hypnotherapist, Leah. Once she had regressed him back to that eventful day at the Holy Ghost hot springs, the first unusual thing that he recalled involved the two pedestrians that had disappeared behind the tree: Both of them had white heads, and an appearance that he could only describe as being "alien" in nature.

The reason for Chuck suddenly becoming overcome by fear was also made apparent: As he was standing outside the VW Bus locking the door, somebody came up behind him. It was the same two beings with the alien-like appearance, and they were preventing him from getting back inside.

Feeling himself inexplicably compelled to do what they wanted, Chuck allowed himself to be taken back the way he had come, walking along the track and past the stagnant pool of water, then up onto a small hill. He was absolutely terrified, but had to go anyway—he was trapped within his own body, devoid of all control of it.

It turned out that the hill's summit was more of a depressed bowl or basin. Nestled within it was a yellow metal spacecraft, resting there on three jointed legs. Rather than being the classic saucer shape, this particular vessel was sleek and tapered to a point; it looked as if it was built for speed, the extraterrestrial equivalent of a dragster.

A flight of steps led up into the interior of the craft. Chuck found himself climbing it, into a chamber that was recognizably a cockpit, complete with pilots' chairs and a host of instruments and controls. The occupants of the craft led him to a table, had him lay down on it, and then drew a sample of blood from him. Surprisingly, the technique was completely painless, something that we haven't yet been able to achieve with twenty-first-century medical technology.

After the blood draw procedure had been completed, the two extraterrestrials escorted Chuck back to his vehicle. Enough time had passed that it was now dark, the bus wouldn't start, and he came close to being killed by the two speeding trucks.

What about the voice that warned him of the impending danger? "It's my guardian angel, or *alien*," he explained to Leah, before going on to explain that an extraterrestrial was watching over him and used telepathy to send him warnings when necessary.

Chuck credits his guardian with saving his life on that lonely stretch of road.

This outdoor encounter has the commonplace "missing time" component to it, but Chuck learned during his hypnotherapy sessions that he has also been abducted numerous times from within the supposed security of his own home.

During one session, Leah was able to take him back in his memories to a time when he was lying on his own bed, gazing up at his bedroom ceiling. A bright, artificial light was streaming in through the windows; the light was actually some type of beam, which caught Chuck in its grip and carried him floating out of the window and up into the extraterrestrial ship.

Chuck described the craft to Leah as being highly reflective, a bluish color, with a domed top and wings on either side. Being outside in the frigid night air quite understandably made him shiver, and as the memory was uncovered for the first time, the present-day Chuck Chroma also began to shiver, causing his hypnotherapist to drape him with a blanket in order to try and warm him up.

Once inside the ship, he was suddenly face to face with an extraterrestrial being, presumably one of the vessel's crew. This wasn't one of the stereotypical Grey entities, however; for one thing, he was taller. This particular being—a boy, with facial features that were noticeably more angular than that of anybody Chuck had ever seen—was a hybrid, a genetic cross between an extraterrestrial and a human. Nevertheless, it was much more extraterrestrial in appearance than humanoid.

Just as Al had experienced during his own encounters, Chuck instinctively knew when he studied his face that this boy had to be his own son.

They were both standing in a long, dark corridor that was lined with what appeared to be glass all along one side. When the boy raised a hand and pointed toward a particular segment of the glass, it was suddenly illuminated from within, revealing the presence of a baby that was floating in liquid, sealed within its own small compartment. An umbilical cord connected to its abdomen was keeping the baby alive, in conjunction with some kind of tubing that entered its mouth—presumably to supply it with air.

A normal reaction to seeing a baby is make cooing, aah-ing noises, but there was nothing pleasant about the sight of this one; Chuck was filled with a sense of revulsion at the doll-like little being. Its facial features were more alien than human.

Unable to help himself, Chuck examined the glass wall more closely. The small subsection housing the baby turned out to be just one of many, with compartment after compartment stacked on top of one another to form the transparent frontage that he had mistakenly thought to be a glass wall at first glance. Each compartment contained a baby, looking different to the one that was now lit up, all variations on a theme. The whole display reminded him of an aquarium.

Why had the boy chosen that specific panel to light up and display to Chuck the infant inside it? It was far from a random choice, the boy said; rather, this baby was also Chuck's, bred from his genetic material. Watching his older son as he said this, Chuck was surprised to find that his lips weren't moving when he spoke. The thoughts were entering his head telepathically.

In an explanation that is frequently given to abductees, Chuck was told that he had been chosen to be part of a massive, noble project, one with the objective of assimilating and incorporating the human race into something larger—*not* to save it. This almost certainly refers to the human/extraterrestrial breeding program that has been spoken of at length by many of those who claim to have been taken aboard alien craft and had their genetic material harvested in order to create hybrid beings.

The reasons for this were straightforward, Chuck's son explained: The human race has devastated its home planet to such a catastrophic extent that it will soon no longer be a viable habitat for life. In order for *something* of humanity to survive, its legacy needed to be a living, breathing one, which would be embodied in the form of the human/extraterrestrials such as himself. They will be the next step in our evolution, albeit an artificially-accelerated one.

When Chuck was returned home after his abduction, he was filled with a sense of incredible loss and great sadness at the thought of his children existing in a place somewhere far away. He hopes that he will one day have the opportunity to see them again.

Chuck found the hypnotic regression session that uncovered this particular encounter to be one of the most difficult and heartbreaking of them all (you may recall that Al reported feeling exactly the same depth of loss when separated from his own hybrid children).

Looking on the positive side, however, he also recounts a feeling of great joy at the knowledge that he has fathered at least two half-human/half-Grey children, who are somewhere out there working toward a higher purpose.

"This knowledge fills me with so much joy, love, and happiness," Chuck explained, "but I was so filled with overwhelming sorrow when I found out that I had to leave them behind, knowing that I couldn't stay and be with them; that I couldn't be around to love, nurture, and take care of them. *It was one of the most powerful, joyful, and yet also one of the most saddening experiences of my entire life.*"

Years later, this deeply emotional experience served as the inspiration for a painting titled *They're Incorporating Us,* which depicts Chuck's encounter with both of his hybrid children in the hallway of the extraterrestrial craft.

One of the pieces of artwork that fascinated me was titled *The Chroma Triptych*. Rather than a conventional painting on a single canvas, this particular piece was oil on three hinged leaves of wood. The *Triptych* conjures up a very Biblical theme, containing as it does the images of the three wise men following a star of Bethlehem that is shaped like an extraterrestrial craft; a robed Virgin Mary laying recumbent on an examination bed in what appears to be an ET craft's control room while three of its inhabitants are gathered around her, conducting a medical exam; and lastly, a Christ-like figure ascending into the night sky on a beam of light that emanates from another extraterrestrial craft.

The beautifully rendered imagery is fascinating, provocative, and will doubtless offend some people as an affront to their beliefs.

"I had wanted to paint this particular piece for many years," Chuck explained enthusiastically. "You see, when I first read the New Testament, I had no idea that I was an abductee—not even the faintest concept. But when I read about things such as walking on water, the resurrection, the star of Bethlehem—especially as it *stood still* over the stable in which Mary and Joseph were staying with the baby Jesus in his manger—well if you take that literally, then there is no way that the star could have actually been a star or a comet. It *had* to have been a ball of light of some sort, and could very easily have been a UFO."

Chuck made it very clear that he intended the painting to be respectful of Christian beliefs and did not want it to be controversial, and strove to portray all of the people and beings depicted with as much dignity and grace as he possibly could.

He wanted to convey a visual sense of being onboard one of the extraterrestrial ships, and used the accounts of other abductees (recovered under hypnosis) that had been published, as a source of inspiration for the painting. One sketch by an abductee named Sandy—a woman who Chuck had never met—looked almost identical to a drawing that he had done himself just a couple of weeks before starting to paint the *Triptych;* both appeared to be drawings of the very same room on an extraterrestrial craft.

That is the room that Chuck chose to immortalize on the center panel of his *Triptych*.

Chuck's last abduction was in 2006, some eleven years ago at the time of our interview. "They tend to be less interested in people as they reach a certain age of maturity," he told me with a self-deprecating laugh, "and with men, it's probably because their sperm count begins to drop and become less viable. The primary reason for abduction was always that: the ability for me to breed."

Although the visitors' interest in him seems to have waned, Chuck has been left with a source of great artistic inspiration, which continues to inject passion into his creative work to this day. If you would like to learn more about Chuck and his art, please visit him at www.chuckchroma.com.

Conclusion
MAKING SENSE OF IT ALL

We—meaning ourselves (human beings) and our extraterrestrial extended family—are fundamentally all one. The universe is essentially one big expression of consciousness to which we all connect. There really is no "us and them." There is only *us*. It is only once one truly begins to accept that notion of universal oneness that a philosophy of absolute kindness and compassion begins to feel mandatory.

For the most part, mankind in its present state is a fundamentally selfish entity when taken overall. While there are those who follow the spiritual path, seeking unity, enlightenment, and placing the good of all over the needs of themselves alone, there are many others who lust after power, fame, influence, and material goods, putting their own selfish desires ahead of the greater good.

The good news is that, in Don and Sierra's considered opinion, the balance is shifting in favor of those who choose to follow the spiritual path. With every day that passes, more and more people are awakening to realize the futility of following the empty road of "me, me, me," and look inward toward the spirit (and outward toward the stars) in search of a higher purpose, something more noble than mere base self-interest.

Humanity as a whole is becoming more and more enlightened with each passing year, and yet ironically becomes less governable as it does so. Although it is now controlled by nebulous forces who in turn control the mainstream media, governmental institutions, and the major corporations, the average human being (if there is such a thing) is growing less and less likely to accept the rule and authority of such overlords. They

Illustration by Chuck Chroma

see a better path—the path of spiritual enlightenment and service to one's fellow man, which leads to a brighter future by far—one in which the old priorities of material excess and the accumulation of wealth hold little or no meaning. Those who say that they have come into contact with alien races report that the more spiritually and ethically advanced ones have essentially outgrown their need for such childish distractions as money and "stuff."

One of the ways in which such growth will be achieved, Don says, is through the development of telepathic communication. This truly will be a game-changer in human affairs. Imagine for just a moment, if you will, a world in which human beings are unable to lie and deceive one another.

Our current political systems would crumble and collapse practically overnight, for one. All are based upon deception, which is used as a means of control and subjugation in many instances. People would be fundamentally more honest. There would no longer be misunderstandings or misinterpretations. Every thought—hopefully controlled and disciplined, for otherwise the consequences could be disastrous—would be "heard" and understood with absolute clarity.

People would treat each other better, simply because there would be no other choice.

This increasing momentum toward spiritual growth and change began in 2012, Don said, when our galactic family came by and "pretty much leveled the playing field." He claims that those more enlightened races finally reached their tolerance threshold and kicked out the more manipulative, less ethical extraterrestrials who were holding the people of the Earth back.

As I sat and listened to Don relate this, it began to ring a bell somewhere in the back of my mind. Leafing back through some of my notes, I found the lengthy section that I had taken during my conversations with Al. He had been told by the extraterrestrials that there was great need for him to continue his healing work during this time of transition. I'd asked him what exactly we were transitioning from and to.

"They didn't say exactly what," he replied, "but they implied that it was some kind of big planetary transformation of consciousness. I can tell you that it began in 2012, and it's picking up speed."

To the very best of my knowledge, Al and Don have never met, and yet they are singing from exactly the same song sheet.

Don went on to tell me that our galactic family isn't going to simply land on the White House lawn (in the best Hollywood traditions) and wave the ET equivalent of a magic wand to make everything better. "They want us to do this for ourselves," he explained, "because to do it any other way would just create a planet-wide codependency, and that doesn't benefit anybody."

This makes eminent sense to me. *Star Trek* fans, of course, know this concept as the Federation's Prime Directive, the general order that prohibits interfering in the affairs of developing cultures. Although there is said to have been an intervention in 2012, this was not done to change the course of humanity's development, but rather to remove malign and manipulative influences from tainting it further.

I asked Don what the ultimate goal of those he refers to as our "star cousins" is.

"They want to see us grow up," he answered. "Right now, it's kind of like parents watching their kids go through the rebellious phase. Now we're starting to mature. They want us to mature and ascend to the higher levels of consciousness and being, and to take our place as a part of the great big galactic family."

When he put it like that, the idea made total sense to me. But it also brought up a rather disturbing prospect, and I framed my next question very carefully. "Part of parenting involves allowing your children to fail, so that they can grow. Usually that means being their safety net, and making sure that those failures aren't *too* catastrophic. But most children aren't destroying their planetary ecology at a frankly shocking rate. Most children aren't armed with nuclear-tipped ICBMs. Just how badly are they willing to allow us to fail, before they *have* to intervene? Or are they willing to throw out the baby with the bath water and allow us to fail to the point of extinction?"

"No, I don't think they'll permit that," Don reassured me. "Nuclear weapons will never again be used. They simply won't allow it. Those weapons rip the fabric of space/time apart and have resulting effects in *their* higher dimensions."

Well, *that* was a relief. I kept thinking back to the Soviet nuclear missile installation in the Ukraine, which had been the scene of the UFO-induced missile arming scare back in 1982. The USA had undergone a similar incident in 1967, at Malmstrom Air Force Base in Montana. After multiple UFO sightings were reported by security teams, a single UFO was seen hovering over one of the missile silos.

One by one, the ICBMs—nuclear missiles aimed at the Soviet Union—began to go off-line, simultaneously shutting down and becoming unresponsive to commands. In human terms, they were falling asleep and refused to wake up. The guidance and control systems, without which the missiles would never make it to their targets in order to deliver their deadly payload, were fully powered up but failed to operate correctly.

Ten of them. One after the other.

The technology behind those nuclear missiles was absolutely state of the art, the end product of billions of dollars' worth of research and development by the finest engineers in the American defense industry. Backups and redundancies abounded. There should have been no way in which such high-tech devices could simply fail to operate . . . and yet they did.

It truly did sound as though the "galactic grown-ups" were sending us the very clear message that such plutonium-tipped mischief would not be tolerated.

"Fortunately, the general population is attaining higher levels of spiritual consciousness," Don laughed. "We're growing up . . . and pretty fast."

Don claims that our solar system has been placed under quarantine by order of the more advanced alien races, who are taking the line that we on Earth need to pull our socks up and solve our own problem. There's really no excuse not to do so, now that the more malign extraterrestrial influences have been taken out of the picture and we have been given a level playing field once more.

In a tone that I hoped did not sound either disrespectful or flippant, I told Don that this was starting to sound like the greatest science fiction-based intergalactic space opera imaginable. My intent was not to mock Don's beliefs (which are shared by many), but I did have to confess that I found the whole thing to be completely mind-boggling. Was it really possible that the humble ball of rock and water that we call home was in fact but one of many population centers in our galaxy?

The more that I thought about it, the more believable it seemed to me. Scientists have discovered many thousands of exoplanets circling around distant stars, each one a potential hub of extraterrestrial life. My mind kept going back to the infamous Drake Equation, as postulated by Dr. Frank Drake in 1961. Drake's equation was one of the first real attempts to codify the number of potential galactic civilizations that may be out there, the components of what some call our "galactic family." Drake's equation factored in the following parameters:

- **The average rate at which stars are formed in our galaxy, and of those stars, how many might possess planets;**

- Of those planets, how many might be capable of supporting some form of life;
- The fraction of those life-bearing planets that actually do give rise to life, and then the fraction of *that* life which is, by our minimum standards, intelligent;
- Of those intelligent civilizations, how many would go on to beam radio signals out into space;
- And finally, over how long a time period would those intelligent civilizations continue to transmit radio waves out into space?

Although Dr. Drake was the first to admit that he intended the equation to be more of a conversational stimulus than a truly objective, hard measure of the number of advanced extraterrestrial civilizations that are out there (and might, therefore, decide to come and visit us, if they became aware of our existence), he couldn't resist plugging in some numbers anyway. The result?

Drake concluded that there could be anywhere between *1,000* and *100 million* such civilizations out there. Now, as amazing as that sounds, many have criticized Drake's numbers, claiming that they lean heavily toward the optimistic side. Others like to point out that mankind has been broadcasting radio signals out into deep space for decades now, and just where exactly are the responses? So far, at least if the official story is to be believed, we have heard zilch. Zip. Nada. Nothing.

And yet, if the witnesses I spoke to and interviewed during the writing of this book are correct (or if even *one of them* is correct) then the possibilities are truly intriguing. We would indeed have all of the necessary ingredients for that "intergalactic space opera."

Volunteers

"This is an extraordinary planet," Sierra interjected, "and human beings were meant to evolve in a certain way, to go on and do great things. But our development has been interfered with, stunted—very deliberately— in order to keep us as dumb as possible, like a herd of cattle."

Sierra and Don are far from alone in their contention that both governments and the mainstream media are complicit in keeping the populace as docile and unquestioning as possible. One only has to look at the contents of the average day's TV programming, pick up one of the more popular "newspapers," or click through the majority of Twitter, Facebook, or other social media feeds, in order to formulate a pretty clear opinion on that.

"So humanity is getting more and more stupid, not to mention docile," I said, taking notes as Sierra talked. She gave me a nod. "It sounds to me as if we're heading for a new dark age, not the great period of spiritual enlightenment that is supposed to have started in 2012."

But apparently my doom and gloom was unfounded. She went on to relate that volunteers have been coming to the Earth in waves for quite some time now, in what sounded to me a lot like some sort of "spiritual D-Day landing." Sierra refers to the work of past-life regressionist Dolores Cannon, who has spent the past twenty-five years delving into the mysteries of the UFO phenomenon.

In her book *The Three Waves of Volunteers and the New Earth,* Dolores recounts the stories of a large number of people who she was able to regress back into a state of being that existed *prior* to their coming to Earth—a non-physical condition in which they experienced life in a state of near-perfect bliss. During the regression process, all of these people (who come from many different countries all around the world) told her that they answered the call to leave their state of joy and happiness, relinquishing something very close to spiritual paradise, in order to help out our beleaguered planet.

This would require them to incarnate in a physical body here on Earth, and to serve in a variety of roles and responsibilities. Some were as straightforward as simply "being" here, spreading positive energy to all those who they encounter during the course of their everyday life. Others said that their assigned task was to observe the events that are unfolding at this critical juncture in the Earth's history.

According to Dolores, the first of the three waves are now close to becoming senior citizens, having incarnated here some sixty years ago. Many of them experienced a severe version of culture shock, finding the Earth so vastly different from their place of origin (it is far meaner, crueler, and more difficult here) that it has been a traumatizing experience for them to come here.

Many of the volunteers who incarnate lose their memories of home, which might explain why members of the second wave of volunteers go through life experiencing a strong sense of loss for something indefinable and intangible. They yearn for another place, a home they have no conscious memory of, yet one that seems to call out to them on a subconscious level. Such people often feel compelled to live alone, rather than deal with the hustle and bustle of society at large, which can often be a disorienting and painful place for them to be.

The third wave of volunteers, many of whom are said to be still arriving now, are said to be comprised of many of the teenagers and children of this current generation. They appear to be coping better with the transition to this material world than those who came before them in the first two waves, and are having a slightly easier time adjusting.

I encourage readers who would like to read more in-depth information on this fascinating subject to seek out Dolores Cannon's book, *The Three Waves of Volunteers and the New Earth*.

Don and Sierra are strong proponents of Dolores' theory that human beings have indeed been stuck in a negative cycle of reincarnation for many, many generations, going through the same life experiences over and over again, and failing to learn much of anything new. We are caught in the quagmire of ignorance and materialistic greed that is partly of our own making, but can also be partly attributed to the malign outside influences (including some of the less ethical extraterrestrial factions) that seek to keep humankind enslaved and subservient.

The way things are *supposed* to work is that we incarnate, learn our lessons, "die," and reincarnate once more to learn different lessons this time around. Each cycle of incarnation *should* bring us closer to our spiritual ideal.

These waves of volunteers are coming onto the Earth from *outside*—most importantly, from outside the cycle of continually messed-up reincarnations. They come from a higher dimension, one of greater spiritual advancement, and are here to act as beacons, exemplars of proper spirituality: rather like lighthouses, showing us the way upward to both enlightenment . . . and the stars.

During the course of our lengthy interview, Sierra told me that she had a strong suspicion regarding what I was. When I asked her what she meant (how could I let a comment like *that* pass?), she smiled and said that my strong compulsion to obtain answers about the paranormal, the UFO phenomenon, and all of their attendant mysteries, is typical of those who came in as volunteers.

I pondered this for a while, and even more so after reading Dolores' book. If what Sierra claimed was true, that would have put me in the second wave of volunteers, whose characteristics are described as being generally focused on helping others (I chose a profession in the field of healthcare), and yet preferring to stay home whenever possible and not mixing often with other people (check—when I'm not at work, I'm happiest sitting at home in relative isolation, tapping away at my keyboard).

Second-wavers are said to deliberately avoid having children (check—my wife Laura and I have never wanted them). What spoke to me the most, however, was the common theme of volunteers feeling a sense of permanent homesickness for a place they have never known, and a disconnection from the modern world. That describes me—and, I suspect, many of you who are reading this book—to a "T." For as long as I can remember, the ordinary comings and goings of everyday life have felt trivial to me, as if there was a bigger picture behind it all that I really couldn't see. Could that explain my lifelong fascination with the paranormal, and why I have spent the past twenty years researching it in both Britain and the United States?

It's an intriguing concept. I cannot say for sure that I personally believe in any of these concepts, but they do fascinate me, and certainly resonate with me on multiple levels. Then again, almost all of us would like to believe that there is more to life than the mundanity of everyday existence; but as I interviewed Don, Sierra, and the other witnesses who have a much different perspective than most, it began to dawn on me just how broad a canvas the story of humanity might truly have been painted on.

So what does it all mean, for you, me, and the rest of the planet? That's the crux of the matter, after all.

Sierra describes the Earth as a living library, a sort of "galactic melting pot," if you will. The Earth was designed and seeded to be home to the very best plants, insects, animals, and indeed pretty much anything that lives or grows, a true biological showcase. She maintains that all of these species were brought here, rather than evolving spontaneously on Earth.

"We have some of the best biodiversity in the entire universe," Don added enthusiastically. This was another mind-blowing concept to me, and my mind jumped to the character of Slartibartfast, the Magrathean designer and builder of planets in Douglas Adams' much-loved *The Hitchhiker's Guide To The Galaxy* saga.

What would those of strong religious beliefs make of it all—was this the equivalent of heresy, incompatible with, say, the beliefs of Christians, Buddhists, Muslims, or any of the other faiths?

Sierra responded to that question by pointing out that she was an Episcopalian minister, and *she* had no trouble accepting it. She finds the theological implications fascinating, and has spent many years studying the various human faiths; it is only now that she has the extra pieces of the jigsaw puzzle in her hands (in the form of the knowledge provided by her contacts with the extraterrestrials) that she truly feels as though the entire picture is in sight.

Much of this comes down to how much the individual is willing to believe. Some of the ideas that Don and Sierra have presented in a very matter-of-fact way will seem outlandish to certain people; yet if one is willing to approach those concepts with an open, enquiring mind, and continues to study the extraterrestrial phenomenon with that same openness, it is my belief that some readers will find themselves deeply enriched by the possibilities that are to be found there.

What do *you* believe?

ACKNOWLEDGMENTS

My heartfelt thanks go out to the following people, without whom this book would never have seen the light of day:

First and foremost, to the wonderful and talented Dinah Roseberry, for opening up the door and inviting me to step through it.

Lucilla Giron kindly shared the story, which has both fascinated and unnerved her family on that night so long ago. Thanks for sharing, Lucilla!

My thanks to Roger Marsh at MUFON, Peter Davenport of the National UFO Reporting Center, and Cammeren Young for graciously giving permission to quote them.

It is impossible for me to adequately express my gratitude to "Al," who patiently laid out his decades' worth of experience—much of it traumatic—and allowed me to share it with the world. Thank you, Al!

Christopher O'Brien, the foremost expert on the enigmatic San Luis Valley, was kind enough to share his insights regarding his experiences there, and his thoughts on the cattle mutilation and UFO phenomenon. I strongly encourage any readers to seek out Christopher's books on the subject, and to connect with him over at *www.ourstrangeplanet.com*.

Judy Messoline took time out to tell me all about the trials and tribulations of building and running a UFO observation station. Thanks Judy! Drop by and see her if you fancy a spot of UFO watching, and visit her on the web at *www.ufowatchtower.com*.

Don Daniels has worked tirelessly for many years on trying to educate the public on his beliefs and principles concerning cosmic citizenry, and how best humanity can develop itself in order to take its place in a broader galactic community. He spent many hours tirelessly explaining concepts to me while on the deck of his mountain home. Readers are encouraged to read Don's book, *Evolution Through Contact: Becoming a Cosmic Galactic Citizen,* and to learn more about his work by visiting www. becomingacosmiccitizen.com.

Thanks are also due to Sierra Neblina, who has poured much of her experience and energy into a program called GalacticU (www.galacticu. com) and GalacticU Radio Network on Blog Talk Radio, in which she works to share the spiritual knowledge and lessons that she has learned with a broader audience, in hopes of helping many people with stories like hers. Sierra is also currently working on a book that will document her life journey in more detail, a project with which I wish her every success.

Tashina Foster, for taking time away from protecting the water at Standing Rock in order to talk about the UFO phenomenon from her own personal perspective. This goes doubly for someone who is generally very shy of the media and likes to stay out of the spotlight. Thank you Tashina!

Joey Stanford, local MUFON investigator, for writing the foreword and giving us a look at the statewide picture. Thanks Joey!

Thank you Chuck Chroma, for your willingness to talk about both your art and your personal abduction experiences. It was very cool to see the two areas of your life converge on canvas. I wish you all the success in the world with future painting projects. Readers can learn more about Chuck's art by visiting *www.chuckchroma.com.*

SELECT BIBLIOGRAPHY

Books

Birnes, William J. *UFO Hunters: Book One.* New York: Tor Books, 2013.

Cannon, Dolores. *The Three Waves of Volunteers and the New Earth.* Huntsville, AR: Ozark Mountain, 2011.

Daniels, Don. *Evolution Through Contact: Becoming a Cosmic Citizen.* Evergreen, CO: ETC Books, 2012.

Hofer, Jordan, and David Barker. *Little Grey Bastards: The Incessant Alien Presence.* Atglen, PA: Schiffer, 2016.

O'Brien, Christopher: *The Mysterious Valley: Astonishing True Stories of UFOs, Animal Mutilation, and Unexplained Phenomena.* New York: St. Martin's, 1996.

O'Brien, Christopher: *Secrets of the Mysterious Valley: An Investigator's Journey through the Unknown.* Kempton, Il: Adventures Unlimited Press, 2007.

O'Brien, Christopher. *Stalking the Herd: Unraveling the Cattle Mutilation Mystery.* Kempton, IL: Adventures Unlimited Press, 2014.

Salla, Michael. *Galactic Diplomacy: Getting to Yes with ET.* Kealakekua, HI: Exopolitics Institute, 2013.

Strohm, Barry. *Aliens Among Us: Exploring Past and Present.* Atglen, PA: Schiffer, 2016.

Web Articles

http://fox13now.com/2014/10/02/unusual-white-dots-spotted-in-utah-skies-after-bright-morning-light-show/

http://legacy.9news.com/story/news/local/2014/10/03/police-investigate-after-ufo-spotted-over-breckenridge/16652997/

http://legacy.9news.com/story/travel/2015/04/01/dia-pranks-conspiracy-theorists-leaked-page/70783916/

www.dailycamera.com/longmont-news/ci_26555260/sky-gazers-spot-google-loon-balloon-over-longmont

www.google.com/loon/how/

www.nuforc.org/webreports/114/S114172.html

www.thedenverchannel.com/news/dia-sculptor-killed-by-own-sculpture

www.ufostalker.com/ufostalker